Pub 12-40

⊘ **W9-AQO-513**

TWAYNE'S WORLD AUTHORS SERIES
A Survey of the World's Literature

Charles Moser
EDITOR

RUSSIA

Vsevolod Garshin

TWAS 627

VSEVOLOD GARSHIN

VSEVOLOD GARSHIN

By Edmund Yarwood

Eastern Washington University

TWAYNE PUBLISHERS

A DIVISION OF G. K. HALL & CO., BOSTON

891.733
G243Y
1981

Published in 1981 by Twayne Publishers,
A Division of G. K. Hall & Co.
All Rights Reserved

Printed on permanent/durable acid-free paper and bound
in the United States of America

First Printing

Portrait of Vsevolod Garshin by I. Repin.

Library of Congress Cataloging in Publication Data

Yarwood, Edmund
Vsevolod Garshin.

(Twayne's world authors series ; TWAS 627 :
Russia)
Bibliography: p. 140–44
Includes index.
1. Garshin, Vsevolod Mikhaîlovich, 1855–1888—
Criticism and interpretation.
PG3460.G3Z94   891.73'3   80-23865
ISBN 0-8057-6469-0

For Craig and Tasha but most of all for Jane

Contents

About the Author

Edmund Yarwood is associate professor of Russian and chairman of the Department of Modern Languages and Literatures at Eastern Washington University. Professor Yarwood has a B.A. and M.A. in Russian from the State University of New York at Albany and a Ph.D. in Russian Literature from the University of North Carolina at Chapel Hill. He has published articles and book reviews dealing with a variety of topics in nineteenth- and twentieth-century Russian literature.

Preface

Vsevolod Mikhailovich Garshin was born in the Ukraine in 1855 and committed suicide thirty-three years later in 1888. Except for a stint in the army (1877–1878) during the war against Turkey and for periodic rests to recuperate from his mental illness (in southern asylums), Garshin spent most of his adult years in St. Petersburg, where his primary occupation was writing.

One of Russia's less prolific writers (his complete works fill one medium volume), he was nevertheless well known to the reading public of the 1870s and 1880s. More than a century after his birth, his fame rests, as it did during his life, exclusively on his stories, especially "Four Days" and "The Red Flower"—two works frequently included in anthologies of Russian short stories. Although he also wrote poetry and art criticism, his efforts in these two genres, mediocre even by the rather modest standards of his contemporaries, contain little of lasting value.

The following brief introduction to Garshin's creative works concentrates almost exclusively on the short stories, examined from a critical-analytical point of view. Much of the critical literature on Garshin is based on a biographical and/or sociopolitical approach. I have sought instead to adopt an intrinsic approach.

I have discarded a chronological presentation in favor of grouping and discussing the stories thematically. Thus Chapter 2 deals with the military stories: "Four Days," "The Coward," "From the Reminiscences of Private Ivanov," "The Action at Ayaslar," "The Orderly and the Officer." Chapter 3 analyzes Garshin's fairy tales: "Attalea princeps," "That Which Never Was," "The Tale of a Toad and a Rose," "The Legend of Proud Aggey," "The Frog Traveler." Chapter 4 presents the art/prostitute tales: "An Occurrence," "Nadezhda Nikolaevna," "The Artists." Chapter 5 is a study of the tales of insanity: "A Night," "The Red Flower"; and Chapter 6 deals with the miscellaneous stories: "The Meeting," "The Bears," "The Signal." I analyze each story separately, but at the end of each chapter I have tried to present the characteristics and traits common to the stories dealing with common themes.

Chapter 7 is an analysis of the basic structure of the Garshinian short story. Garshin structures each story on the interaction of two focal points—one occupied by a hero, the other by a foil. The hero is a type, a nervous, introspective, lachrymose individual, often goalless, often manipulated. In an attempt to understand his own life, the hero verbalizes his own experience; so that the stories are frequently told from his point of view. Offsetting the hero is a foil. The foil elicits responses from the hero, offers him alternatives, forces him to act or otherwise causes him to respond to external stimuli. Since the stories are often psychological, the hero responds more in the inner world of thought than in the outer world of action.

Garshin began writing his short stories in the late 1870s, at a time when the dominant genre in Russian literature was the novel which reached its apogee at the very end of that decade with Leo Tolstoy's publication of *Anna Karenina* (1878) and Fedor Dostoevsky's publication of *The Brothers Karamazov* (1880). Like the other nascent writers of this era, Garshin was subject to the influence of Tolstoy, Ivan Turgenev, and Dostoevsky (Chapter 8), but he still made some original contributions to the development of the short story in its newly emerging form—for example, his use of the hero-foil interplay to create inner tension and his use of the devices of Impressionism.

Garshin was definitely instrumental in popularizing the short story, though Anton Chekhov caused this genre to replace the novel in *fin de siècle* Russia. While Chekhov would be credited with almost every innovation in the short story, many of his innovations had been standard elements in Garshin's stories (Chapter 9).

I would like to thank those without whose help the present study would never have been completed, especially: Paul Debreczeny of the University of North Carolina, who introduced me to Garshin and under whose direction I wrote my dissertation (the main ideas of which are presented in Chapter 7); Eastern Washington University for granting me a sabbatical leave to work on the manuscript; Charles Moser, editor, Russian Section, Twayne's World Authors Series, whose perceptive and helpful criticism greatly improved my study; and my wife, Jane, for her excellent editorial comments and her patience.

EDMUND YARWOOD

Eastern Washington University

Chronology

CHAPTER 1

Life

I *Early Years*

VSEVOLOD Mikhailovich Garshin was born on February 2, 1885[1], in the Bakhmutsky District of Ekaterinoslav Province in the Ukraine. The Garshins were members of the impoverished nobility whose roots went back to the fifteenth century, though the family had little information, oral or written, about its origins other than the fact that an ancestor, Gorsha (or Garsha), a member of the Golden Horde, had converted to Russian Orthodoxy and received land in the Voronezh Province.

Vsevolod's paternal grandfather, Egor Arkhipovich, possessed the most negative traits of the nobility: he frequently availed himself of the *jus primae noctis;* he was cruel, inflexible, and physically abusive when dealing with his peasants; he exasperated his noble neighbors by involving them in endless legal actions over trivial matters. This last trait caused his potentially profitable estate to deteriorate to the point at which Vsevolod's father, Mikhail Egorovich, one of eleven or twelve children, inherited only seventy serfs, or as they were more appropriately termed at that time, "souls."

In many respects Mikhail was the opposite of his father. A quiet, unprepossessing, rather weak man, he finished the *gymnasium* and studied two years at Moscow University before choosing a career in the military. Here, he also distinguished himself by his mild temperament, refusing, for example, to use physical force, i.e., beatings, to punish his soldiers, a rarity in the Russia of Nicholas I (ruled 1825–55).

While traveling with his regiment in the Ukraine, Mikhail became acquainted with Ekaterina Stepanovna Akimova, the daughter of a Bakhmutsky landowner, and married her in 1848. Ekaterina's father and Garshin's maternal grandfather, Stepan, was a most un-

13

usual man for his times—educated, kind, gentle, sympathetic to his peasants. With such traits in common, it is apparent why Mikhail and Stepan liked each other. Stepan was, however, disliked by his fellow landowners, who initially looked upon him with suspicion and took him to be a free thinking liberal. Subsequently, however, after he mortgaged his estate to buy bread for his serfs, who were dying of hunger during the famine of 1843, they considered him merely insane.

Vsevolod's personality and psychological makeup reflected the influence of his maternal grandfather and his father. His intellectual development and interest in literature were to show the influence of his mother.

Ekaterina Stepanova, the eldest of five daughters, was in Garshin's words "a well educated girl for that time and for the remote expanses of Ekaterinoslav Province, an exceptionally well educated person."[2] The military life with its constant moving about obviously greatly appealed to Ekaterina, for it enabled her to meet and speak with a continually changing stream of people. For Vsevolod, the third of three sons born to Ekaterina and Mikhail, on the contrary, this type of life was decidedly unsettling. In a short autobiographical sketch written later on, Garshin looked back to this time and recalled his impressions as a three-year-old: "As through a dream I remember the regimental life, the huge red horses and huge men in armor with blue and white jackets and fur caps. We often traveled together with the regiment and I have preserved in my memory of this time many troubled reminiscences."[3]

In 1858 Egor died; with his small inheritance Mikhail bought a home in the city of Starobelsk, located eight miles from the Akimov estate, and retired from the military. The military memories died slowly for the Garshins, however. Vsevolod woke up one morning in his fourth year and took leave of his mother to go to war, telling her: "Good-bye, Mama. What's one to do? All must serve."[4]

Mikhail relived his military career in endless retellings of the battles of Sevastopol, in endless recountings, now exaggerated, now embellished, of military experiences. Ekaterina, the "exceptionally well educated" provincial woman, endured this static, uneventful life for two years. Then, unable to bear it any longer, she left for St. Petersburg with her lover, the revolutionary Peter V. Zavadsky, taking with her her two older sons but leaving Vsevolod with his father. St. Petersburg, Russia's cosmopolitan and Western capital, was admirably suited to Ekaterina's personality, but the effect of her departure on the five-year-old Vsevolod was devastating (Garshin has left a pathetic but touching portrayal of this period in his story "Noch' " [A Night]). After three years she took Vsevolod back, but the psychological damage had already been done. As Garshin comments in his autobiography: "The predominantly sad expression on my face probably began during this period."[5]

In 1864 Garshin enrolled at a *gymnasium* in St. Petersburg. Though we know little of his experiences there, his two favorite subjects were composition and natural sciences, both of which were influential in his literary career. He never lost his interest in natural sciences, and his stories are filled with numerous and specific references to Russian flora and fauna. In addition, among his best and closest friends Garshin numbered Alexander Gerd, a naturalist, and Victor Fausek, a zoologist.

During these early *gymnasium* years, Vsevolod lived at home. Conditions were not always the best there, but he was at least with his mother and three brothers—Evgeny, the fourth Garshin son, having been born in 1861. Whether the father was Mikhail or Zavadsky only Ekaterina (and perhaps not even she) knew for sure. Vsevolod throughout his life was a close and devoted brother to Evgeny; he was thus disappointed when his mother moved to Starobelsk with Evgeny, leaving him to make do on his own.

Physically and psychologically these were difficult times for Vsevolod. Near the end of 1872 he began to be afflicted with the mental illness which was to plague him for his entire short life. Hospitalized with a nervous breakdown, he at first seemed to improve to the point where he was about to teach the other inmates English, but his illness worsened in early 1873 to such an extent that he was forbidden all visitors. As he slowly recovered he was allowed to leave the hospital, but the strain was too much and he was forced to move to the convalescent home of Dr. Alexander Frey. By summer of 1873 the illness had passed, and in the fall Garshin resumed his studies. In this same year he learned that his older brother Victor had committed suicide, a tragedy which would strike the Garshin family more than once.

Forced to live with several different families during these years, plagued by financial worries, concerned over his pitiable father and his domineering, jealous mother, Vsevolod completed the seven-year *gymnasium* program not in 1871, but in 1874. He expressed his feelings during this period in a *cri de coeur* to his mother: "Oh, Mama, how miserable I am. I can't even cry anywhere: I don't have a corner of my own."[6]

During these years of torment and isolation, Vsevolod found consolation in literature. A prodigious reader from the time his mother first left him, he escaped the realities of life in the realms of fiction. Having completed the *gymnasium,* but unable to enter the university, he matriculated at the Mining Institute in the fall of 1874. He spent the summer before this pleasurably in Starobelsk, where he became good friends with Raisa Alexandrova, a musician and music teacher. Her family took a great liking to him, as did Raisa, and they maintained a close and tender friendship for several years; her sisters and friends staged Gogol's play *The Marriage,* and the summer passed pleasantly and quickly.

In contrast, the next two years at the Mining Institute dragged by slowly. Vsevolod knew he was not destined to be a mining engineer, and so spent much of his time in other areas, viz., art and literature. He became friends with a group of artists and frequented their gatherings, called "Fridays." His interest in this area led him to contribute seven articles on art to St. Petersburg journals between 1877 and 1887, and provided him with background information which would later prove invaluable in his stories dealing with art.

He also began to write. At first he tried his hand at poetry, but found he was not inspired in this genre. "Having forsaken poetry, I will not forsake prose," he wrote to his mother in January of 1875.[7] And he was true to his word, though writing took longer and came harder than he had thought it would. He vowed to Raisa in September of 1875: "I promise you that this winter you will see my name in print. I must take this road at all costs."[8]

Keeping his promise, Garshin wrote a satirical sketch of a town council meeting in a provincial town, obviously modeled on Starobelsk, "Podlinnaia istoriia Enskogo Zemskogo sobraniia" (The True Story of a Zemstvo Meeting in the Town of N***). He took the sketch to Alexey Suvorin, the well-known editor of the popular newspaper *Novoe vreuya* (New Time), who appraised the work favorably but tactfully suggested Garshin submit it to the lesser-known journal *Molva* (Town Talk). Garshin did so, but instead of signing it with his own name signed it R. A., for Raisa Alexandrova.

Their many contacts from 1874 to 1876 make it clear that Raisa and Vsevolod were strongly attracted to each other, and their friends expected a marriage announcement as a matter of course. However, they did not marry. Neither Vsevolod nor Raisa nor Ekaterina ever explained why a break occurred, though Garshin's mother, a jealous and possessive woman, might certainly have played a role in separating the couple. Or perhaps, as Raisa's sister believed, the history of insanity in the Garshin family proved too great a hurdle for the prospective marriage.[9]

On March 3, 1876, Vsevolod received a letter from Apollon Zhemchuzhnikov, the editor of *Molva*, telling him his "True Story" would be published. He was ecstatic: "My rejoicing knows no bounds. The sketch is very short, microscopic, but, you know, this is my first published work. I feel the same way my favorite, Master David Copperfield, did when his article was accepted."[10]

II *War and Literature*

As spring turned to summer, another stimulus appeared in Vsevolod's life to distract him from his studies—the Balkan situation. Ferment and revolt had been the order of the day there since 1875, with the Herzegovinians, Bosnians, and Bulgarians rebelling against the Turks. In the summer of 1876 Serbia declared war on Turkey, an action which aroused great sympathy and fiery, though mixed, support in Russia.

Garshin, now near the end of his second year in the Mining Institute, tried to enlist in the Serbian army to help that Slavic country in its struggle with the Turks, but he was rejected because he was not of military age. The next year, on April 12, however, Russia entered the war on the side of the Serbs, and Garshin, with a friend from the institute, Vasily Afanasev, immediately enlisted as a volunteer. Like the hero of his story "Trus" (The Coward), Garshin had mixed feelings about joining. He knew, on the one hand, that war was the cause of untold misery and countless deaths; and yet, on the other hand, he felt a need to share this suffering. That April he wrote to his mother: "Mama, I can't hide behind the walls of the Institute while others my age are offering their breasts to bullets."[11]

Despite his rather delicate nature, Vsevolod endured the physical and psychological hardships of war rather well, was well liked by his fellow soldiers even though he was a gentleman *(barin)*, and

was less terrified by it all than he had imagined he would be. On
the contrary, in many ways his short tenure in the army had a
positive psychological effect on him. The regimentation, the physical exertion, and the lack of time for free thought prevented Garshin
from reverting to the melancholia of his student days.

On two occasions Garshin saw action against the Turks. The first
occasion was merely a minor skirmish at Eserdzhi, but the second,
the battle at Ayaslar on August 11, 1877, was more serious. While
attacking, a column of Russian soldiers was thrown back and forced
to retreat. Vsevolod, with his line of vision partially obscured, did
not notice the slight retreat and was cut off from his fellow soldiers.
When the troops recognized Vsevolod's predicament, the Russian
line advanced and soon he was once more in the midst of friends.
Just at that moment he was felled by a bullet in the leg.

Removed to a military hospital, Garshin had his wound treated.
Though it was not serious, it healed slowly because the bullet had
torn off a chunk of flesh. He recuperated first in Bela, in Bulgaria,
and then in St. Petersburg. Thus ended Garshin's short military
career. His bravery in battle, however, did cause him to be recommended for a medal.

Garshin's military service had a profound effect on his literary
career. "As I expected, the material for observation has turned out
to be endless. If God endures, I will know what to do. I have almost
no doubts that I will be able to write and will be successful."[12]

His prophecy was borne out, for Garshin did write and was successful, especially with his military stories, and most notably "Che-
tyre dnia" (Four Days), which caused a sensation in Russia.

From Bela Garshin was moved to Kharkov, where he spent two
months recovering in his mother's apartment, but the steady stream
of friends, well-wishers, and curious visitors tired him so that he
moved to St. Petersburg in December, as soon as he could manage
on crutches.

Russia's capital welcomed Vsevolod as a new literary star: he was
bombarded with requests from newspapers and journals for stories.
But the new year, instead of being joyous, proved to be difficult,
and Garshin was in a quandary about his literary and military future.
As to the former, despite his popularity he published only two short
works in 1878—"Proishestvie" (An Occurrence) and "Ochen' ko-
roten'kii roman" (A Very Short Romance). As he explained in that
year: "I will now publish only in extreme cases. I am writing, it's

true, a sufficiently large amount, but all these are, for me, studies, exercises. I have no desire to submit them although I am sure they would appear not without success."[13] Apparently—since he was now better known and widely read—Garshin was more cautious of his future literary reputation.

As to the military, he wavered over what to do. He considered making the army his career, but when he was recommended for a medal and promoted to ensign in the spring of 1878, he worried about having to serve again: "Although I have been crippled till now, they suddenly pronounce me healthy and I'm ordered to Vidden. In my current state of health (nerves) this is for me a death sentence. . . . I'm in a bad way: I'm depressed because I can't do anything; I don't do anything because I'm depressed."[14]

By autumn he had decided to leave the army. After a battery of tests in a St. Petersburg military hospital, he received a disability discharge.

Most of the next year was taken up in reading, writing, and visiting friends in the provinces until fall, when he again suffered a nervous breakdown. Over the following two years his mental state was unpredictable, with periods of sanity alternating with periods of insanity.

On February 20, 1880, a young radical, Ippolit Mlodetsky, attempted to assassinate Count Mikhail Loris-Melikov, the extremely powerful, conservative head of the Supreme Executive Commission formed earlier that year by Alexander II (ruled 1855–1881). Mlodetsky was apprehended and tried by a military court, which sentenced him to death.

Garshin was tremendously upset by the incident, and obtained a night-time interview with Loris-Melikov to plead for mercy for Mlodetsky. He left thinking that his entreaties had achieved the desired result, but evidently Loris-Melikov, conscious of the mental state of his wild-eyed visitor, allowed him to believe that his wish would be granted. The next day Mlodetsky was hanged.[15]

After this Garshin went on a wild tour, now appearing in Moscow, now in Kharkov, now in Tula. In the course of his travels, he suddenly appeared at Yasnaya Polyana, the estate of Leo Tolstoy, to discuss good and evil with the great writer, who, prior to this meeting, had known neither Garshin nor his literary work. Leaving as abruptly as he had arrived, he set off with a Bible to preach forgiveness among the peasants in their villages. Eventually he was found in one of these villages by Evgeny, who took him back to Kharkov.

Vsevolod spent three weeks there, but suddenly vanished, only to reappear in an insane asylum in Orel. He was returned to Kharkov once again, where he was ensconced in an insane asylum, the Saburov Dacha, for several months before being transferred to Dr. Frey's convalescent home in St. Petersburg. Ultimately he wound up (from the end of 1880 to the spring of 1882) at the estate of his uncle, Vladimir S. Akimov, in Kherson province.[16] Akimov strictly regulated Vsevolod's activities during this period, believing that order and regimentation were the best medicine for his nephew. In May of 1882 Vsevolod, against his uncle's advice, returned to St. Petersburg and slowly resumed his literary activities. Most particularly, he collected those stories which had been previously published in journals into a book. That volume of stories brought Garshin to the attention of Ivan Turgenev.

That summer Turgenev invited Garshin to his estate, Spasskoe. Garshin accepted the invitation and spent the summer there writing "Iz vospominanii riadovogo Ivanova" (From the Reminiscences of Pvt. Ivanov). Due to illness Turgenev himself was not there during Garshin's stay. While the two writers occasionally corresponded, they never met in person. Garshin admired Turgenev greatly and dedicated his most famous story, "Krasnyi tsvetok" (The Red Flower), to him at the time of his death.

That fall, having decided to refrain from "making literature the sole occupation"[17] of his life, Vsevolod found employment for several months in a very minor position before becoming secretary in the office of the Congress of Representatives for Russia's railroad industry. He was to keep this job almost until his death and found it much to his liking, for, except during sessions of the Congress, when he would be very busy, most of the year he was only required to be in the office for three hours a day. This gave him time to write and pursue other activities.

One such activity was his marriage in February 1883 to Nadezhda Mikhaylovna Zolotilova. Vsevolod had become acquainted with Nadezhda six years previously when recuperating from his wound. Their friendship had gradually developed into a deep love, culminating in their marriage. Nadezhda, a medical student at the time of the wedding, shortly thereafter completed her studies and became a doctor. Garshin's marriage to Nadezhda brought him immense joy and profound grief; joy, for she was affectionate, tender, loving, and (thanks to her medical background) understanding of Vsevolod's mental illness; grief, for he knew that his bouts with insanity tormented her. In a letter to his friend Fausek he wrote: "I have been horribly depressed the past six months by the most frightful, groundless depression and I greatly fear that I will become ill. Dying is not so horrible to me as falling ill. And if Nadezhda Mikhaylovna were not near me, I would undoubtedly fall ill."[18]

Though the previous two years had been happy ones, 1884 proved to be dismal. In that year the government closed down *Otechest-vennye zapiski* (Notes of the Fatherland), the popular and prominent journal which had served as the chief mouthpiece for the Russian populists. Garshin had published the majority of his stories in this periodical, knew the editorial staff, and was dismayed to learn of its demise. In this same year he also underwent another period of deep depression. For the next four years these periods would inexorably appear in the spring/summer.

At times the fits of depression would drive him to the edge of the abyss, as he wrote to his friend Vladimir Latkin in 1885: "I have often bitterly regretted that the bullet eight years ago did not turn a little more to the left. What kind of life is this: eternal fear, eternal shame before loved ones whose life you have poisoned. Why does Nadia [Nadezhda] have to endure such grief. . . . I never wanted to die as much as now. I, of course, don't contemplate suicide: that would be the ultimate act of baseness."[19]

III *The Last Years*

From winter 1886 to spring 1887, Garshin's psychological state improved to the point that his friends commented that their old friend was back. During Easter he took a two-week trip to the Crimea with a friend and his daughter. His letters home to Nadezhda are cheerful and talkative, the letters of a psychologically sound person. This pleasant period was shortlived, however, and from the summer of 1887 through the winter of 1888 he was despondent. Many factors affected him in his final nine months. His periodic bouts with insanity had caused him to miss work frequently, and despite the fact that his employer was kind, Garshin felt it best for all concerned to give up his position. The spare time this afforded him was not beneficial to him.

When Semyou Nadson, a popular poet and friend of Garshin's, died, Garshin attended the funeral but was in an extremely agitated state before, during, and after the event.

Perhaps the most trying episodes of this time, however, involved family problems. His brother Evgeny had married Nadezhda's sister, but the marriage was of short duration. Garshin's mother blamed her newest daughter-in-law, of course, and when Nadezhda intervened on her sister's behalf she also incurred her mother-in-law's wrath. Vsevolod defended his wife and received his mother's curse as a result. Throughout his life, Vsevolod had catered to his whimsical mother's wishes, always backing down in a dispute even when he knew he was right, so as not to provoke her. Thus her curse was a blow to him. This, on top of everything else, caused Vsevolod to feel that his world was crumbling, and he rushed to see Dr. Frey, his trusted friend and doctor. It was felt that a trip away from St. Petersburg should be the first step in easing Garshin's troubled spirit.

On March 20, 1888, before he could leave, and despite what he had written to Latkin in 1885, Vsevolod Garshin threw himself down a flight of stairs. On March 24 he was dead.[20]

His funeral on March 26 drew several thousand spectators, in a fitting tribute to his popularity and success.

CHAPTER 2

The Military Tales

I "Four Days" (1877)

"FOUR Days" was the first important work Garshin published. Begun in Bela while he was recuperating from his wound and finished shortly thereafter in Kharkov, the story was submitted to *Otechestvennye zapiski,* which immediately accepted it for publication. The story was immensely popular, appearing as it did at the height of the Russo-Turkish War, and overnight Garshin became a literary success. The story recounts the experiences of a Russian soldier who, wounded in battle, must lie next to the body of a Turkish soldier he has killed. For four days the soldier undergoes mental and physical torment as he watches his victim steadily decompose while he ponders his life and his act. At one point he hears voices, but is afraid to call out for fear the voices may be Turkish, not Russian; by the time he realizes they are friend, not foe, it is too late and the opportunity is lost. Sustained by water in his victim's flask, the soldier endures and is eventually rescued.

The idea for "Four Days" was provided by a true incident which befell Garshin during his short military service. The fictionalized presentation was based on the experiences of a soldier, Vasily Arsenev, described in a quotation from the *Kratkaia Istoriia 138-go pekhotnogo Bolkhovskogo polka* (The Short History of the 138th Bolkhovskii Infantry Regiment).

Four days after the Eserdzhinsky battle [in Bulgaria in 1877] our regiment's second battalion was sent to bury the dead. Having finished its work, the battalion moved back and, passing in a line through the bushes, accidentally discovered in a dense thicket, a wounded soldier, a private of the second infantry company, Vasily Arsenev.

The unfortunate soldier was wounded in both legs and had been lying helplessly for four days and nights. After administering to him, they happily

23

carried him to the regiment and then to the hospital. There Arsenev related how, lying in the bushes, he often heard voices, but could not make up his mind to shout out, not knowing whether they were Turks or Russians.

—I lived—the wounded soldier reported—on water from a flask taken from a dead Turk lying next to me. The hunger and the pain in my legs were tolerable, but the most horrible thing of all was the odor of my neighbor—the Turk, who was already decomposing from the heat. Private Arsenev nevertheless was unable to recover and in a short period of time died.[1]

Garshin's purpose in writing "Four Days" was to show, in general, the horrors of war, and also, through the device of introspection, to show, in particular, an incident of war as experienced by a simple soldier. Since the story is presented as an inner monologue, the reader sees all events (with the exception of the conclusion) through the soldier's eyes. The opening paragraph is presented as a remembrance—the words "I remember" are repeated four times in the opening—in which the narrator, in the present, thinks back on events in the past. The reader learns that the narrator had entered into combat with a Turk who was physically superior to him: "He was a huge, fat Turk, but I ran directly at him although I am weak and thin" (3).[2] He kills the Turk and races on until everything disappears. The physical clash between the narrator and the Turk is a prelude[3] to the main part of the story: Ivanov's mental and physical suffering while lying next to the body of his victim.

Garshin is careful to show that, when Ivanov awakens after the battle, though he is confused, he is capable of rational thought. He wonders if his wounds are fatal, if the Turks defeated the Russians, why he wasn't picked up with the dead and the wounded. He answers his own questions when he determines that he has been wounded in both legs; he logically reasons that the Turks were not victorious; he comes to the rational conclusion that he was not taken away because he was hidden by the bushes.

When he sees the body next to him, however, he becomes anxious and afraid: "Help! Help!" (5); "Oh, grief, grief! You are worse than the wounds" (7). The next morning, in the light of day, he realizes the body lying next to him is the corpse of the Turk, and the corpse becomes a symbol both of war in general and of Ivanov's act in particular. At first Ivanov can associate with his victim as a counterpart of himself: he sees him as a simple soldier brought by fate to the war; he wonders whether the Turk, too, has an old mother.

He feels that he, himself, is innocent of evil—"I don't want this. I didn't wish evil to anyone when I came to fight" (7)—and his victim is even less guilty. The Turk evokes ambivalent feelings in Ivanov, who must bear the responsibility for his act. He has murdered the Turk and yet he feels no hatred for his alleged enemy. He wonders: "Why is he to blame? And why am I to blame even if I killed him?" (8), but these questions he cannot answer.

The Turk is the living embodiment, *mutatis mutandis,* of Ivanov's crime, but he also becomes a symbol of life and death for him: life, for Ivanov survives thanks to the water in his victim's flask; death, in that the Turk's rifle is lying nearby and makes suicide a possible alternative—"One need only stretch out a hand; then—one second, and it's over"(8).

Ivanov refuses the latter alternative and chooses life, albeit a life of physical and mental torment on the field of battle. Part of his ordeal lies in watching the decomposition of the Turk. In three separate descriptions, each emphasizing to a greater extent than the preceding one the nonhuman characteristics of the corpse through the use of metaphors and other tropes, the reader is introduced to this aspect of war: "His face was already gone. It had slid from the bones. A horrible bony smile, the eternal smile, appeared to me so negative, so horrible. . . . This is war, I thought, here is its manifestation . . . "(12).

In the end, Lazarus-like after four days, the soldier is brought back to life and taken to a hospital, where in the last scene the reader observes the amputation of his leg by a "noted St. Petersburg professor" (14).[4]

II *"The Coward"* (1879)

"The Coward" appeared in *Otechestvennye zapiski,* subtitled "From a Notebook," after Garshin had reworked the story to suit the censors. The title of the work refers to the narrator, who does not wish to serve in the war, for he sees its senselessness and absurdity. Faced with the moral dilemma of serving or not serving, a problem perceived, at first, on an abstract and philosophical plane, the nameless narrator is forced to witness the slow death from gangrene of his friend Kuzma Fomich. The narrator is thus forced to view the general threat of death and war through the prism of the specific death of his friend. Kuzma faces his inevitable death almost calmly, with the woman he loves, Marya Petrovna, staying by his side throughout his ordeal. The narrator in the end allows himself to be inducted into the army, where he is eventually killed by a stray bullet while his unit is held in reserve.

From the opening paragraph it is evident that the narrator's overriding concern—at least in the beginning of the story—is with the war as it personally affects him. When elevating war from a specific encounter to a generalization on man's militaristic bent, the narrator is worried not so much by the fact that man is militant, as by the possibility that man's militancy will directly involve him and those near to him: "It seems to me that the current war is only the beginning of future wars from which neither I, nor my young brother, nor my sister's infant son will escape" (33).

He feels more involved with the war, he believes that it affects him more than others, that others accept newspaper descriptions of the carnage "calmly" while he suffers torment after reading them. At first he views the war from a position of relative security, believing that because he is in the militia he will not see action. This complacency, however, is shattered by Lvov, Marya Petrovna's brother, who informs him that even the militia will certainly be called up. This forces the narrator to perceive his situation in a new light. The question of serving in the war and perhaps dying now becomes a very real problem to him.

Using the same deductive device, Garshin first presents Kuzma as ill with a toothache, a minor physical discomfort; later the toothache is replaced by gangrene, a usually fatal illness in nineteenth-century Russia. Thus Kuzma is also compelled to change his perspective.

The story ebbs and flows along two constantly intertwining lines, one involving Kuzma, the other the narrator. Of course, since the story is related in the first person from the coward's point of view, both lines of development are subjectively linked to him. The narrator who doesn't want to participate in the carnage of war, an action initiated intentionally by men, is obliged to interact with Kuzma, a chance victim of fate: "Kuzma seems to me a unit, one of those of whom there are tens of thousands mentioned in the reports" (40). He has a great effect on the narrator's thoughts and actions, for until the onset of Kuzma's illness the narrator is concerned only with himself. Kuzma's illness forces a change in the narrator—he is compelled to get involved. Garshin demonstrates this through the use of the word "sacrifice." Thus the doctor asks Kuzma whether he has any friends who could sacrifice some time for him. Earlier Lvov has castigated the narrator for fruitlessly reflecting on war instead of choosing a course of action which would help his fellow man, telling him that at such times one must sacrifice oneself. The narrator is, of course, one of those who will help Kuzma, and through this sacrifice he will reconsider his own situation. For him Kuzma comes to represent in microcosm the macrocosm of war.

The narrator's dilemma is compounded by the fact that he has the option of utilizing "certain influential acquaintances" to remain in St. Petersburg, an option he does not exercise because an "inner voice" tells him it is not right. At this point the reader and the narrator learn that Kuzma is suffering from gangrene and all the concerned characters in the story know that he will not survive, that his death is imminent. The narrator discerns a parallel between his friend's fate and his own. After hearing Kuzma's plaintive cry: "I don't want to die!", he thinks to himself: "I don't want to die and none of these thousands [at war] wants to die either" (42). A parallel exists between his own and Kuzma's life, but the narrator notes that the circumstances are not the same: "Kuzma at least has found consolation at the last minute—but there [i.e., at the front]? Death will always be death, but to die among those near and dear to you, or falling in the mud, in your own blood, expecting that at any moment someone will come up and finish you off, or that a cannon will run over you crushing you like a worm . . . " (42).

Despite his fear of war and of dying, the narrator is eventually taken into the army willingly, partly through the intervention of Marya Petrovna, who speaks to him of war as a "*general* grief, a *general* suffering" (44).[5]

The narrator goes to war, but while waiting for his train to leave he is informed by Lvov and his sister that Kuzma has died. With these words, the narrator's notebook ends and the story is continued by an omniscient narrator, who describes a field of battle, a battalion in reserve, and the death of a *barin* (a member of the gentry, presumably the coward/narrator) by a stray bullet. Thus the narrator's life ends by chance, as had Kuzma's.

There is a degree of irony in this ending, for the coward/narrator has been connected with death on two previous occasions. In the first, Lvov tells a story of an officer who hangs himself because he cannot accept the suffering around him. Lvov, connecting the narrator's mental state with the officer's, warns the narrator: "If they don't kill you—you will go out of your mind or put a bullet through your head" (47). He is partly right—the narrator does get a bullet in the head, but he faces his death calmly, like Kuzma, not hysterically, like the officer in Ivov's digression.

The second digression is related by "the young soldier with the cheerful face," who tells about the young *barin* who, when the fighting starts, discards his rifle and knapsack and runs away. A stray bullet hits him in the back as he flees.

The present *barin* (i.e., the coward/narrator) assures the young officer that he will not behave the same way, and indeed he does not, for a stray bullet punctuates the officer's story by striking the "*barin*/listener," killing him instantly.

So in the end the narrator shares Kuzma's fate. Garshin accentuates the connection by ending the story with the word for wound (opening)—*otverstie*—the same word used to describe Kuzma earlier in the work. Through the influence of his friends, especially Kuzma, the narrator comes to accept his participation in the war and his death with serenity.

III   *"The Orderly and the Officer"* (1880)

"Denshchik i ofitser" (The Orderly and the Officer) was originally intended to be the first of a series of sketches dealing with military life entitled *Liudi i voina* (People and War). Except for the first sketch, the envisioned project was left undone.[6] As a result, "The Orderly and the Officer" has little plot, action, or movement; instead it is a comment on military life as developed through two character portraits—the orderly Nikita, and the officer Alexander Mikhaylovich Stebelkov.

The reader is introduced to Nikita in the beginning of the work through a multi-faceted portrait. First Nikita is presented from a physical point of view. The narrator remarks that those who maintain there is nothing more beautiful than the human body would have recanted upon seeing Nikita standing naked during a military physical examination. The author's lengthy description of Nikita's physical oddities is capped by a colonel's comment: "Ape!"

From the physical the author moves to Nikita's family position. Nikita's loss will obviously have a devastating effect on his family's well-being, for they will be left with no men in the family save the elderly Ivan. Moreover, Ivan's natural son has died the year before, leaving an extra family to be cared for.

Garshin describes the effect on Nikita of being called up in one sentence. "God alone knows how this week passed for Nikita, because he remained silent the whole time, preserving on his face the same set expression of submissive despair" (121).

In presenting Nikita in relation to his family, Garshin, rather like Chekhov, uses selected details, allowing the reader to complete the picture by filling in additional details. Though little is actually stated, much is communicated.

Nikita's private life then becomes a foil for his life in the military. Though of great value in his private sphere, Nikita is absolutely incompetent and worthless as a soldier. Attempts to train him come to naught. For a year and a half he is given the least desirable and most miserable assignments (124). Nikita's situation changes only when a new officer, Stebelkov, appears in the regiment.

Stebelkov is everything Nikita is not, from his pride in his magnificently pointed mustache to his contentment with military life. In the ensuing presentation of Nikita and Stebelkov, both come across as stupid, but Stebelkov revels in his inanity and views his career as a lieutenant as a reward for his early, turbulent, poverty-stricken life.

He thus revels in the hours he spends in bed rereading back issues of the popular magazine *Niva* (Cornfield). He enjoys his aimless life and forces Nikita to lead a life without substance also. When Nikita engages in surreptitious cobbling to pass the time, Stebelkov eventually discovers his activity and prohibits it. Nikita must lead a life of "compulsory idleness" *(obiazatel'noe nichegonedelan'e).*

Garshin clearly depicts the contrast between the relationship of past, present, and future of both characters in the dream sequences which conclude the stories. Each dream begins with the same words—"The wind drones and howls, the snowflakes beat against the window. And it seems to the sleeping . . . " (130–31). The subsequent dreams, however, are quite different. To the sleeping Stebelkov the storm seems to be "the thunder of ballroom music" (130). He sees himself at a ball where all treat him with respect and admiration. He looks at his shoulders and sees a general's epaulettes. He moves from the ball to a field of battle where he dispenses advice to all around him. The dream ends with monsters rushing at him, and with his crying out for Nikita.

For Nikita the storm seems to be a real storm. He imagines he is in a hut all alone. When he calls out, all his village acquaintances appear and point out to Nikita his family; Nikita realizes at this point that his family and friends are all dead. At first the dead pursue him, but they are replaced by Lt. Stebelkov, who runs after him calling his name.

It develops that Stebelkov is really calling his name because he needs matches to light his cigarette. After stumbling around in the dark, Nikita finds the matches and gives them to Stebelkov. Within a quarter of an hour both the officer and the orderly are asleep again.

IV   *"From the Reminiscences of Private Ivanov"* (1883)

Stebelkov appears also in "From the Reminiscences of Private Ivanov," though here in a minor role. The two major roles in this work are played by Ivanov, the narrator, and an officer, Ventsel. The story consists largely of a series of scenes describing life in the army, although the scenes are described in a manner one student has termed "almost epic in its serenity and sweep."[7] Only several scenes depict the interaction between Ivanov and Ventsel; yet these scenes are vital for they serve as the thread which connects and unifies the work as a whole.

Private Ivanov, though educated and of the same class as the officers, refuses an offer to move out of his tent with the peasant soldiers into theirs. Ventsel chides him for his concern for the peasant, a concern Ventsel apparently does not share: as the narrative progresses, several scenes depict Ventsel's cruelty toward the peasants. The narrator, intervening when Ventsel is beating a soldier, also incurs the officer's wrath. As the story ends, however, Ventsel is weeping bitterly over the loss of half of the soldiers in his company, a fact which forces us to reevaluate our perception of him.

Private Ivanov is a naive, inexperienced soldier, and though we follow the campaign through his eyes from the day he arrives to enlist through the battle scene in which Ventsel loses his men, he himself is never involved in military action.

As a newly enlisted soldier, the narrator relates events in a detailed, specific manner, emphasizing their uniqueness for him. This may be illustrated by the story's first paragraph:

On May 4, 1877, I arrived in Kishinev and within half an hour I had learned that the 56th Infantry Division was passing through the town. As I had come with the goal of enlisting in some regiment and going to war, on May 7 at four o'clock in the morning, I was standing in the street among the gray ranks which had formed in front of the quarters of the Colonel of the 222nd Starobelsky Infantry Regiment. I was wearing a gray overcoat with red shoulder straps and blue facings and a kepi with a blue band. I had a knapsack on my back, cartridge-pouches at my waist, and a Krynkov rifle in my hands. (137)

The specificity of detail and the freshness of the scene as perceived by the narrator serve to transform an otherwise ordinary setting into something unique.[8] As the narrator becomes more attuned to his new life and becomes part of a larger group, the narrative voice occasionally changes from "I" to "we." Part of the author's intent is to enable the reader to follow Private Ivanov's military education, a slow process which causes the reader to sympathize with the narrator. Thus Ivanov, who at first has trouble differentiating twenty-two-year-old Fedorov from forty-year-old Uncle Zhitkov, later cannot comprehend how he could have possibly mixed up the two.

The narrator forms a bridge between the common soldiers and the officers. He has an affinity with the former because of his rank, and with the latter because of his class. He is, however, not really comfortable with either because of his education. Captain Zaikin comments on his own lack of education compared to Ivanov; Ivanov's superiority over the soldiers is evidenced in an incident when he corrects a soldier who mistakes Bokhara for Bulgaria. Actually it is only with Ventsel that Ivanov is intellectually and educationally on a par. At their first meeting they discuss literature and Ventsel recites French poetry, which causes Ivanov to comment that Ventsel "read well: simply and expressively and with a good French accent" (147). On the subject of the peasant, though, the two are in disagreement. Ivanov respects his peasant soldier friends; Ventsel believes that they understand only one thing—a fist.

From this kernel of contention develops the conflict between the two. Ivanov at first vacillates between two perceptions of Ventsel:

from his direct contact with him he believes Ventsel to be a sensitive, intelligent individual; but his indirect information—i.e., hearsay from Fedorov and Zhitkov—is that Ventsel is a harsh, unfair taskmaster. This dichotomy of character is maintained in a scene in which Ventsel approaches Ivanov on a march, exchanges amenities with him, shares his water, and takes leave of him. Shortly after this exchange, when Ivanov witnesses Ventsel beating a soldier with his scabbard, he intervenes to halt the beating. Ventsel is by now completely transformed: "He turned an infuriated face toward me. He was terrifying with his eyes rolling in his head and his mouth convulsively distorted" (151). And instead of being applauded for his heroic action, Ivanov is criticized both by Ventsel and by Zhitkov.

Later on, when Ventsel again beats a soldier, Zhitkov prevents Ivanov from intervening, but not from observing the scene and describing it in detail. Zhitkov, however, implies the soldiers will take revenge in the first battle, a hint the narrator undertakes not to comprehend.

Near the end of the work Ventsel and Ivanov have their last confrontation as they examine the bodies of two soldiers killed in action. Ventsel asks Ivanov his opinion, and Ivanov responds in a rage that they will no longer be bullied and beaten since they are no longer soldiers, but people. To that Ventsel replies, "They are people. . . . Dead people" (176).

These selected scenes, however, do not form a cumulative harsh portrait of Ventsel. On the contrary, the final scene, with Ventsel "sobbing bitterly," takes the reader aback. Our sympathy is with him and we realize our belief that he lacks concern for his soldiers has been wrong. Ventsel's bravery in leading his men into combat, coupled with his grief for those who have been lost, forces us now to reconsider his actions. Ventsel, leading his men on five successive charges, is one of the heroes of the day. The Turks, it turns out, outnumber the Russians three to one, but Russian courage, as witnessed in the specific example of Ventsel, convinces the Turks that the Russian forces are stronger than they really are. The narrator, in constrast, is not tested under fire.

Ultimately, then, there is no resolution to the story. We, as readers, are compelled to recognize the complexity of Ventsel's character, and the original judgment we make of him is altered. Human nature, like war, is complex and unpredictable.

V *"The Action at Ayaslar"* (1877)

As we already know, Garshin was involved in the Battle of Ayaslar:
it was there he was cut off from his fellow soldiers and there that
he suffered his leg wound. Out of these personal experiences he
composed the sketch "Ayaslarskoe delo" (The Action at Ayaslar),
which often reads more like a war correspondent's account than a
work of fiction. Told from a first-person-plural point of view, the
sketch details the everyday life of the soldiers; though the work
builds toward the final battle scene, there is no plot. Neither un-
derplaying nor overplaying the life of a soldier, the narrator instead
depicts life realistically, both with its exciting moments (the battle
scenes) and its boring periods: "Camp life passes listlessly, monotonously, when there is nothing to do and when one is in the middle
of nowhere it is even worse" (384).

Structurally the work consists of scenes from military life strung
together and loosely connected by the narrator. The scenes include
a forced march, a discussion of the importance of knapsacks, an
observation of a skirmish, a description of the boredom and anxiety
of soldiers awaiting battle, the preparations necessary for doing
battle, and finally the battle scene itself.

The uniqueness of the sketch derives from the narrator's unro-
manticized observations and impressions, which he frequently presents through eyes seeing them for the first time, so that the reader
participates and is educated along with the narrator. The emphasis
is not placed on the battle, but on the preparations for it; not on
heroic attacks, but on soldiers returning to the rear after having run
out of ammunition in battle; not on close-ups of hand-to-hand combat, but on the distant employment of military methods: "I lay firing
now and then, occasionally getting advice from Pavel Ignatevich
(our corporal) on the height of the sights and asking whether or not
we should fire on chance at the artillery" (397). The final battle
scene is largely autobiographical, for the work ends with the wound-
ing of the narrator.

Overall "The Action at Ayaslar" as a story of war is, thanks to its
realistic presentation, more chilling than Garshin's fiction. The descriptions of the disintegrating corpse in "Four Days" are indeed
horrible, but so too are the matter-of-fact descriptions of the narrator
at Ayaslar, who frequently alludes to the silence as well as the noise
of battle: "Those lying down would occasionally wildly shout out,

those standing behind the trees would fall to their knees sometimes with a shout, sometimes silently. Gavrilo Vasilich, who had only just arrived and was loading his rifle, fell forward, a shell fragment had hit him in the groin, tearing out his innards. Those of the wounded who were able to crawled away, for the most part, silently; or perhaps their cries could not be heard due to the noise of battle" (397). Ironically, the sounds of war are most noticeable for the narrator when he is not directly involved in battle. It is while waiting in reserve that he hears them most clearly.

As he was to do later in "From the Reminiscences of Private Ivanov," in "The Action at Ayaslar" Garshin concentrates on establishing a mood, an atmosphere. He emphasizes the drudgery of war. Men seem to act in slow motion because, in part, of the stifling weather conditions. Intermixed with the day-to-day depictions of the prosaic there is, however, a touch of poetry. The author describes twinkling stars, the smell of mint, moonlight: "The tops of the poplars started to turn white; the leaves turned silver and shone with the soft reflection of moonlight" (392).

VI   *General Characteristics*

Garshin's attitude toward war was ambivalent, and this ambivalence is reflected in his stories. While he was aware of the senselessness of war, he nevertheless volunteered for action, feeling, as does Marya Petrovna in "The Coward," a need to participate in the "general grief," the "general suffering." Grief and suffering are concomitant elements of all the military tales; in each it is the psychological rather than the physical suffering which is most difficult to bear. Certainly Ivanov in "Four Days" suffers physically from the wounds in his legs, but the result of his act torments him most. As a matter of fact, the most gruesome descriptions center not on Ivanov's wounds, but on the Turk's. The narrator in "The Coward" dies as a result of the war, but this is in the closing scene, an unexpected one. The story concentrates rather on his psychological torment in coming to grips with the war. Likewise Nikita does not suffer physically—instead he welcomes the hard, dirty labor inflicted on him as a punishment, for this frees him from the vocal and psychological abuse of the officers. Even in "The Reminiscences of Private Ivanov," where physical abuse does occur, it pales beside the psychological torment experienced by the narrator in witnessing and recording that abuse.

Like many writers, Garshin deals with the impact of war on individuals, and in so doing he emphasizes its senselessness. Nikita does not want to participate in the war; he does not want to leave his family, where he is highly regarded and valuable as a person, but he has no choice. Garshin underlines the fact that Nikita is the only able-bodied young man to provide support for three families. Yet what happens to his life? He is brought to a point where it has lost all meaning and value. Stebelkov, a stickler for order and form, refuses Nikita permission to engage in a useful occupation—repairing boots—and his life lapses into long periods of sleep intermixed with the running of foolish errands for Stebelkov.

The war fails to have meaning for any of the heroes. Indeed they are tormented by the war, and although they participate in it they never seem to understand why they should. They are drawn into the action and are swept along by it. The protagonists in the military stories share certain characteristics possessed by Garshin himself: they are introspective, self-effacing, sensitive individuals who feel they must participate in war just because war is horrible and they must share the common suffering. The heroes are passive beings who go to die, not to kill. The hero of "Four Days" explains: "The thought that I would have to kill people never occurred to me. I only imagined how *I* would offer my *own* breast to the bullets" (7).[9] Likewise the narrator in "From the Reminiscences of Private Ivanov" remarks that in battle "it is necessary to kill, or rather, to die" (180).

Death does occur, of course, but the depictions of death are presented not in raging battle scenes, but in places disassociated from the violence of war and often after the actual battle scenes. The narrator in "The Coward" hears about Kuzma's death while waiting for a train, and he himself is killed by a stray bullet while his unit is held in reserve; Ivanov kills the Turk in a battle scene, but he is unaware of his act and describes the battle rather impressionistically—only later when the battle is long over and he is isolated from the arena of action does he describe the corpse of his victim; in "From the Reminiscences of Private Ivanov" we do not witness the deaths of Ventsel's men, but rather the effect those deaths have on him after the fact.

In the final analysis there is almost no action in these stories and certainly no military action. Garshin had no inclination toward jingoism, preferring to depict the conflict internally, in the minds of his heroes, rather than on the field of battle, with the result that he underplayed the military nature of war. We see, by and large, soldiers reacting not in combat, but on marches, in reserve, on bivouac, etc.

War in these stories seems to have no purpose. One soldier loses a leg without understanding why; another weeps over his men who have fallen in battle, but the reason for their death is neither given nor implied by the author; another is reluctantly drawn into the military but is killed waiting to go into battle.

In his military stories, as in most of his prose works, Garshin is primarily concerned with effect rather than cause. His narrators are involved in an ongoing process of experiencing events, not just recording them. If the tales are related by a first-person narrator, it is because Garshin wants the reader to follow not acts and actions themselves, but the effect these acts and actions have on the narrator. His narrators are acute observers and their impressions are vitally important, since his protagonists are not men of action but men of perception.

CHAPTER 3

The Fairy Tales

I "Attalea princeps" (1880)

"ATTALEA princeps" appeared in *Russkoe bogatstvo* (Russian Wealth) after *Otechestvennye zapiski* rejected it as too pessimistic. The story takes place in a greenhouse in Russia. The plants housed there are indigenous to tropical climes and frequently engage each other in arguments over the state of affairs in their new environment. The largest of all the inhabitants—a Brazilian palm given the scientific name of Attalea princeps by the botanist who is director of the greenhouse—becomes disgusted by the constant bickering of those around her and exhorts them to grow and grow until they shatter the walls of the greenhouse and achieve freedom. When the others refuse, she undertakes the task alone, or rather with the aid of a pitiful herb. She succeeds in breaking through the roof of the greenhouse, but is then cut down at the director's orders and thrown into the back yard along with the herb.

From the story's opening paragraph we are struck by the dichotomy between appearance and reality. The omniscient narrator describes the greenhouse as unusually large and beautiful, a structure of iron and glass with spiral columns and ornamental arches, which becomes even more beautiful during a sunset, when "the whole building would sparkle and red reflections would gambol and play as though in a huge, finely cut gem" (92).

All is not so beautiful within the greenhouse, however. Despite the size of the building, the plants are crowded inside—roots interweave with roots, branches grow against branches and bend against the cold glass panes, where they snap off or are pruned by the greenhouse workers. This closeness causes friction among the inhabitants of the structure, who engage in daily arguments.

The tensions mount for yet another reason: the plants' present world is not their real world. The greenhouse is specifically designed

37

to provide shelter for plants which otherwise could not survive the harsh Russian climate. Thus the plants live in a cramped, artificial environment, deprived of tender breezes, of direct sunlight, of freedom: "The plants needed space, their native land, and freedom. They were natives of tropical lands, tender, luxurious creations: they remembered their homelands and longed for them" (92).

Attalea princeps, more than any of the others, feels this longing, and this is one of several ways in which Garshin sets the title character apart from her fellow plants. She is also more beautiful and taller (by over ten meters) than the others; the others group together and are jealous of her, while she is alone and proud; she is nearest to the glass roof and the blue sky and thus more aware of the outside world. Her yearning is intensified by a visitor to the greenhouse from her native land who becomes melancholy while gazing at her, touching her, thinking about his travels: "And he remembered that he had not been happy anywhere except in his native land, though he had traveled around the whole world" (94). The next day he leaves for Brazil, an option not open to Attalea, of course.

Instead, she seeks freedom by the use of force. When the others fail to support her plan to unite to break the iron framework of the greenhouse, she decides to go it alone. A most worthless and pitiful herb, used only for ground cover, goes along with the palm: the most proud and the most humble are thus united for their task.

Although there is a degree of hostility between Attalea and the others, her real nemesis is the greenhouse director. A prototype of Chekhov's man in a shell, the director has retreated into physical and psychological encasement. In contrast to the palm, who seeks to break out, the director is not only happily encapsulated in his greenhouse, he even works within a glass booth located inside the glass house.

Psychologically, too, the director has found refuge within the laws of science. When the Brazilian visitor uses the palm's Brazilian name, the director tells him that its name is Attalea princeps. The visitor replies that although its scientific name may be Attalea princeps, its real name is the one he has used. The director's retort tells us much about his nature: " 'Its real name is that which science has given it,' the botanist drily said, and locked the door of his little booth so that he would not be disturbed by people who did not understand that if a man of science said something, it was necessary to be silent and listen" (93).

As Attalea grows larger and larger in her attempt to break through the roof, the director takes the credit for the fact that the tree has reached heights not attainable in her native land. Watching her grow, he sometimes strikes her with his walking stick, causing her leaves to shake from the blow, whereas the Brazilian visitor touches her gently.

While the director's arrogance bothers Attalea, she is scarcely any less arrogant herself. As she reaches the top, "the cold framework pierced the tender young leaves, cut through them and deformed them, but the tree was obstinate" (98). When the herb expresses pity for the pain her companion is undergoing, Attalea responds: "Be silent, weak plant! Don't pity me! I will die or I will be free!" (98).

At the very moment of this speech Attalea succeeds in crashing through the roof, shattering glass and metal. The crux of the story is now reached, for instead of the joy she had expected to experience when she had attained freedom, she finds the harsh, fatal reality of a snowy Russian day: " 'Only this?' she thought. 'It is only for this that I languished and suffered so long?' " (98).[1]

She realizes that all is over. Her experience of the world outside makes life within the greenhouse appealing: "She had to stand in the cold wind, to feel its gusts and the sharp touch of snowflakes, to look at the dirty sky, at indigent nature, at the dirty back yard of the botanical garden" (98). The director orders her to be cut down and thrown into the back yard. The herb is ripped out and tossed on top of her.

Soviet critics have interpreted the disparity between the illusion and reality of freedom which Attalea finds in the story as an allegory of nineteenth-century Russian autocracy. For example, Sergey Shuvalov, a postrevolutionary critic, comments that "investigators see in the story an allegorical portrayal of the heroic and hopeless (in [Garshin's] opinion) struggle of the revolutionary terrorists with tsarism."[2]

In viewing the story as a criticism of nineteenth-century Russian autocracy, Soviet critics perhaps misinterpret an image used by Garshin in a poem dealing with the same topic—i.e., a palm tree who breaks out of a greenhouse—"Plennitsa" (The Prisoner, 1876). The relevant line goes as follows: "Ot dereva tsarskii venets otdelili" (They detached the royal crown from the tree) (370). Garshin's intent in the poem, however, is clearly to use *tsarskii* in its general meaning of "royal" as opposed to its more specific meaning of "relating to the tsar."

II "That Which Never Was" (1882)

"To Chego ne bylo" (That Which Never Was) is a light, ironic tale in which Garshin pokes fun at human narrow-mindedness and self-satisfaction, aspects of a larger failing called by the Russians *poshlost*; (banality), a word often employed in Russian literary criticism.[3] The story begins on a hot June day, when most of the inhabitants of a farm are resting after a midday meal. The tale is built around a conversation involving a disparate group: a snail, an ant, a dung beetle, a lizard, a caterpillar, a grasshopper, a bay horse, and two flies. Each takes part in the conversation and expresses an opinion, though one limited by the speaker's narrow, self-centered point of view. The lizard is unable to interject its opinion because Anton, a coachman, inadvertently dispatches the gathering with his foot, in the process breaking off the lizard's tail. The lizard later remarks on the loss of her tail, after which the author makes a final closing comment.

The dung beetle begins discussing the purpose of life by opining that one's role in life revolves around one's posterity: "Life is work for a future generation" (133). When a new beetle appears, it feels that it has done all that was expected of it.

A toiling ant interrupts at this point to criticize the dung beetle's labor, which has as its aim merely the reproduction and preservation of the species. The ant sees its function as nobler, as labor for the *bien public*. It works despite the heat, despite the fact that no one will appreciate its efforts. The ant admits that it doesn't know what compels it to act the way it does, only that it is unhappy, but must work nevertheless. Its closing comment, however, seems to ally it with the dung beetle: "Fate!" (134).

The grasshopper now chirps in that they are not dealing with the original question—"What is the world?" (134). It sees the world in physical terms—sun, grass, breezes—and berates its companions who have no conception of its immensity. The grasshopper brags of her jumping abilities, which enable her to see "that the world is without end" (134).

The bay supports this statement, regretting that the others are unable to comprehend a word like "verst."[4] The horse, however, seems merely to want to talk for the sake of talking. In discussing places it has been, the bay is more interested in the food it received there than with any philosophy of space.

The snail finds the bay's statements about distances incomprehensible. Having spent four days on one burdock, it can find no reason to travel farther than to the nearest plant. What is joy to the grasshopper is nonsense to the snail: "It is not necessary to jump anywhere—all this is imagination and nonsense" (135). A caterpillar interjects into the conversation a statement on its future life as a butterfly, and two flies comment nonchalantly on losing their mother in a jar of jam.

The lizard, who had posed the original question—What is the world?—begins to offer an opinion, though he also decides that all opinions offered so far have been completely correct! Just as it commences to argue its own point of view, in apparent opposition to the aforementioned "correct" ones ("But on the other hand"[135]), it loses its tail to Anton, who destroys the entire company with the exception of the two flies.

The lizard's tail grows back, but is never quite the same. When others ask how it lost its tail, the lizard replies: "They tore it off because I decided to express my opinion" (136). One of the main purposes of this blatantly ironic story is to lead up to the two final statements: one the lizard's, the other the author's, whose final comment on the lizard is—"and she was absolutely correct" (136).

In writing the tale Garshin set out to parody certain topical beliefs. Shuvalov, for example, mentions that "it is not difficult to recognize certain social theories of the time, which are presented as a subtle parody."[5] The intent of the story notwithstanding, the work is still enjoyable to read and relevant to our own times, because the various viewpoints set forth are universal, archetypal ones which show us how narrow and egocentric our worlds really are.

III   *"The Tale of a Toad and a Rose"* (1884)

According to his friend Victor Fausek, the idea for the "Skazka o zhabe i o roze," (Tale of a Toad and a Rose,) came to Garshin during a musical evening. "Rubinstein was playing," he recalled, "and directly across from Rubinstein was sitting and staring fixedly at him a highly unattractive old man of high rank (now deceased) with an unpleasant appearance. Garshin looked at them both and, as an antithesis to Rubinstein and the listener sitting opposite to him, the idea about the toad and the rose flashed in Garshin's mind."[6]

The tale, subtitled "For Children" when it was first published, tells of the experiences of a beautiful rose blooming on a sunny day and of an ugly toad who desires to eat her. Interwoven into this conflict is the story of a dying boy whose sister plucks the rose for him at his request.

The work begins with a stock Russian fairy-tale opening—"There lived in the world" (*Zhili na svete*). The rose's environment is then described in some detail; the state of the flower bed in which it grows, with its overgrown weeds, rotting trellises, unkempt pathways, discarded garden stakes, tells us much about the past and present condition of the country house and its inhabitants. Undaunted by their surroundings, the flowers flourish. Among them is a bush on which, one bright May morning, a rose appears. The rose serves as a symbol of beauty in the work and is described in tender terms—thin, pink petals covered with tears of dew, a delicate scent of perfume.

The symbol of ugliness—the toad—is next presented in terms designed to arouse revulsion in the reader: "It used to sit, its toad eyes covered with a membrane, almost imperceptibly breathing, expanding its dirty-gray, wart-covered, sticky sides, and having put one deformed paw to the side, it was too lazy to move it to its belly" (218).

The physical oppositions are extended to the environment in which each is pictured: the rose is always presented in the bright, clear air, the toad on the damp, cool soil.

Once the toad catches sight of the rose, it proclaims its intention of gobbling it up, while the rose, unable to escape, can only wish for some other death. The toad is unsuccessful in its first attack, for it cannot withstand the rose's thorns; during the second attack the rose is saved by the boy's sister.

The toad/rose theme is clearly linked with the brother/sister theme. Garshin quite deliberately establishes a connection between the boy and the toad. "Last year during the fall *on that very day*[7] when the toad found itself a fine chink under one of the stones of the foundation of the house . . . the little boy came to the flower garden for the last time" (218).

Garshin also establishes a connection between the boy and the rose when his sister tells him: "There is a rose which has blossomed just for you and what a glorious one it is" (222). The connection between the two is maintained in their respective deaths. The sister snips the rose for her brother, dislodging the attacking toad in the process. The sight of the rose brings a smile to the boy's face; after smelling it and exclaiming, "Oh, how wonderful" (222), he dies. His exclamation contrasts with his sister's, who, upon seeing the toad, cries: "Oh, what a horror" (223).

The presence of death at the end of the work convinced one critic, Dmitry Moldavsky, that the moral of the tale is that "death conquers all,"[8] but this interpretation is difficult to accept. To be sure, the rose dies, but she feels "that she was not plucked in vain" (223), for she dies bringing a smile to the young boy's face. She fears not death per se, but death at the hands of the toad. The normal life of a rose, the author tells us, is three days; yet at the end of the story we are informed by a first-person narrator (who has supplanted the previous third-person narrator) that "When she began to wilt, they placed her in a thick old book and dried her out, and then, many years later, they gave her to me" (223).

The point is, quite simply, that the rose survives for many years rather than three days, that her death was not pointless but purposeful, and that her life therefore had meaning and value.

IV *"The Legend of Proud Aggey"* (1886)

Garshin took the idea for the "Skazanie o gordom Aggee" (The Legend of Proud Aggey,) from an old Russian legend, "The Tale of the Soulworthiness of Tsar Aggey: How He Suffered Because of His Pride," which had appeared in two collections of folktales: Alexander Afanasev's famous *Narodnye russkie legendy* (1860), and Alexander Veselovsky's *Razyskaniiakh v oblasti russkogo dukhovnogo stikha* (1881). The legend was a popular one, and Leo Tolstoy happened to be reworking it at approximately the same time. In a letter of April 6, 1886, Vladimir Chertkov, Tolstoy's friend and secretary, informed him that Garshin was working on a story based on this legend,[9] and Tolstoy then abandoned his version.[10]

In Garshin's variant a rich king is all powerful and alone. Once upon hearing a priest read a passage from the Bible stating that "the rich will become poor and the poor will become rich," he becomes enraged and has the priest imprisoned and the page ripped out of the Bible. God intervenes at this point: and while occupying the king with a stag hunt, he sends an angel in the guise of Aggey to replace him. After some trying experiences Aggey realizes what has happened, runs into the deep woods, weeps, and is not heard from for three years. After ruling for three years, the angel-king invites all the poor and wretched of his kingdom to his palace for a feast, at which the real Aggey appears, serving as a guide for twelve blind men. The angel tells Aggey his period of punishment is over and he may once again assume the mantle of power. Aggey prefers, however, to continue his life as a guide for the blind. After three days the angel returns to heaven and the body he has occupied is laid to rest by the people of the kingdom, who believe their king has died.

Garshin subtitled his story "A Retelling of an Ancient Legend," and incorporated many traits of folktale and legend into his work. These include standard openings ("Once upon a time there lived in the world" [*Zhila-byla na svete*]); standard epithets ("the clear field" [*chistoe pole*]); repetition (*bil-bil*); the use of *da* as a conjunction; trebling; hyperbole; the standard feast (*pir*); and others.

Garshin's version is fairly true to the original, though a major deviation occurs in the conclusion. In the original, King Aggey, after his three years of atonement, accepts the scepter and mantle once again, while Garshin's king prefers to devote his life to the blind men. In view of Garshin's other works this change is not surprising. In almost every story he wrote, Garshin endowed his heroes with certain common traits. These heroes are highly moral, self-effacing, nonaggressive self-sacrificers highly sensitive to good and evil, more concerned with justice and spiritual integrity than with material power.

Rare is the hero who does not exhibit these traits. Once such, however, is the frog-traveler.

V *"The Frog Traveler"* (1887)

The hero of "Liagushka-puteshestvennitsa" (The Frog Traveler) is a frog who, after conversing with a flock of ducks, expresses a desire to join them in their flight south. The frog invents a method of transportation: she will hang by her mouth from a stick held between the beaks of two ducks. This means of conveyance works admirably until people below comment on this miraculous event.

Afraid that people will think the ducks had invented this praise-worthy system, the frog cries out to them "It is I! I!" (311). As soon as she opens her mouth, of course, she falls to the ground.

In this as in his other tales, Garshin's "point" is apparent. Garshin's tales are not allegories of profound moral, social, or philosophical import; rather they are didactic tales designed to point up a moral, but done in a light manner.

In "The Frog Traveler," as in several other tales, the ending is ironic. Garshin is not vicious in his conclusions, for the frog does not plummet to her death as a result of her desire for praise and recognition. Rather she lands in a new swamp where, obviously not having learned a thing from her encounter with the ducks, she tells the astonished frogs around her "a miraculous story of how she had pondered her whole life and finally invented a new, unusual means of traveling by ducks" (312). Once she has begun, she cannot stop bragging and fabricates a tissue of lies about her life in the south, her flock of personal ducks, her reasons for landing in this new territory, etc.

Garshin often added subtitles to his tales in an attempt to convince his readers that these tales were for children—"Attalea princeps (A Tale)," "The Tale of a Toad and a Rose (For Children)"—and although Garshin himself stated that his tales were simple children's stories, the evidence points to another conclusion. Speaking of "That Which Never Was," for instance, Garshin tells his friend Fausek: "I had no thought in mind that one could imagine that these Antons . . . or flies were other than flies and Antons."[11] To be sure, the characters in the tale are not allegorical symbols used by the author in place of specific persons or specific philosophies; and yet, taken as a whole, the tale does portray a negative facet of man's character, and the irony of the narrative belies any claim that the tale was truly intended for children.

The fact that Garshin published most of his tales in adult journals further weakens any contention that he wrote them for children. While "The Frog Traveler" appeared in the children's magazine *Rodnik* (The Source), "Attalea princeps" came out in *Russkoe bogatstvo* and "The Tale of Proud Aggey" was published in *Russkaya mysl* (Russian Thought). Garshin wrote his tales for adults, among whom they were quite popular. Even the revolutionary youth of the time enjoyed them.[12]

The fairy tale gave Garshin a great deal of latitude, since verisimilitude is not a mark of the genre. He was not, for example, comfortable in depicting human nature ironically and/or negatively. In the fairy tales he could overcome this hesitancy by using the device of anthropomorphism. Chekhov was a master at portraying man's foibles, but Garshin was not, and so resorted to depicting human failings in a frog or an ant or a dung beetle. In addition to their ironic elements, the fairy tales enabled Garshin to create strong-willed, arrogant, assertive characters such as Attalea princeps or King Aggey and villainous characters such as the toad or the botanist/director.

Most important, however, the fairy tale enabled Garshin to be didactic and moralistic. Each fairy tale conveys a lesson to the reader, and the author formulates his ideas as simplistically as possible. Thus, in contrast to the psychologically introspective, first-person narratives of the military tales, the fairy tales are third-person narratives with a heavy reliance on external detail and outer appearance. Their external settings differ from the inner ones of his other works; they depict sharply defined, clearly delineated, black and white worlds. There is no ambiguity in the fairy tales, no oscillation on the protagonist's (or antagonist's) part: the rose is good, the toad, evil; King Aggey is evil and arrogant before he sees the light, loving and humble afterwards; the frog is a braggart and nothing will change this; the botanist/director's narrow perception of the world is subject to no alteration.

Though they were plainly meant to be tendentious, the fairy tales should not be read too seriously, since Garshin sprinkles them liberally with humor, especially ironic humor, which is so decidedly lacking in all his other works. It was as if the author's own experiences with life—his melancholia, his periods of insanity—caused him to view the all too real world as tragic and humorless, while humor and laughter could only exist in the world of make-believe.

CHAPTER 4

The Artist and the Prostitute

I Art Criticism

V SEVOLOD Garshin had an abiding interest in art. While most of his artistic endeavors were in the area of fiction, he did publish seven articles on art in the course of his life. Four of these appeared in 1877 in the journal *Novosti* (News), and all four display Garshin's preference for the "Peredvizhniki" (Wanderers) school of art over the Academy school of art. The St. Petersburg Academy of Art, founded in 1754 by Catherine the Great, was the dominant force in Russian art from the Academy's inception to 1870. Outdated, bureaucratic, academic, the Academy promoted an art-for-art's sake philosophy in a Neo-classical framework. Each year artists entered the Academy's Gold Medal competition by submitting works on an assigned topic, one typically chosen by the Academy from among biblical, Classical, or mythological subjects. The Academy viewed its topics as morally uplifting and ennobling, but many artists of the time found them restrictive and stultifying.

In 1863, when the Academy announced its competition would consist of works on the theme of "The Banquet of the Gods in Valhalla," thirteen artists and one sculptor refused to enter the competition and broke off from the parent institution to establish their own art society. By 1870 this group, the Society for Wandering Art Exhibitions—so called because of its wandering exhibits which toured from town to town and village to village in an attempt to bring art to the people—was a powerful rival to the Academy. Strongly utilitarian in their approach to art, the Wanderers believed that art should be concerned with, though subordinate to, reality. Convinced that art could and should play an important role in social reform, they were careful to paint on subjects which would arouse sympathy and compassion for the common man—the peasant in the country and, later, the worker in the city.

The call for socially useful art had been issued several years earlier, in 1855, when the radical critic Nikolay Chernyshevsky published his famous essay "Esteticheskie otnosheniia iskusstva k
deistvitel'nosti" (The Aesthetic Relations of Art to Reality). Chernyshevsky and his close followers were concerned solely with content, and cared little for the form used to transmit it. Among the
Wanderers and their sympathizers there was also a great concern
for socially useful content, but the better artists were also vitally
concerned with form and technique and succeeded in maintaining
high creative artistic standards.

That Garshin, with his own concern for the common man, with
a social message in his works, should feel an affinity for the Wanderers is not surprising. In his first published art criticism, "Vtoraia
vystavka 'Obshchestva vystavok khudozhestvennykh proizvedenii' "
(The Second Exhibition of "The Society of Art Exhibitions"), Garshin displays his prejudices before he even begins discussing the
exhibition. For example, he mentions that the "Society" a year
before had tried to imitate the success of the "Wanderers" by staging
its own exhibition. This attempt had failed, Garshin writes, and so
he ascends the granite steps of the Academy in a despondent state
of mind as he prepares to visit their second exhibition. Having set
the stage for another failure, he finds fault with most of its works
of art, often in stingingly ironic tones: "Our venerable coryphaeus,
Mr. Ayvazovsky, has exhibited six (why not sixty?) paintings, if it's
possible to call our respected professor's creative products by such
a name" (317).

Despite the predominantly negative tone of his article, Garshin
does single out one painting, *The Return of the Sacred Carpet from
Mecca to Cairo* by Konstantin Makovsky, for special praise, re-
marking that this one painting nearly compensated for the generally
depressing impression left by the exhibition as a whole.

As a postscript to his article, Garshin mentions the fact that several
of Ilya Repin's paintings are also hanging in the academy, although
not listed in the "Society's" catalog. Garshin feels that the "Society"
is taking advantage of Repin's fame by making it appear that Repin
is one of them, when in fact he was closely aligned with the Wanderers. One of the finest Russian painters of the nineteenth century,
Repin became a close friend of Garshin's, who even sat for him,
posing as Ivan the Terrible's son in Repin's *Ivan IV with the Body
of His Son.*

In the late 1880s Garshin projected a series of articles of Repin's significance in the history of Russian art, but the plan never came to fruition.

Garshin's second article, "Novaia kartina Semiradskogo 'Svetochi khristianstva'" (Semiradsky's New Painting "The Lights of Christianity"), is devoted to the description of a single work, albeit a massive and complex one depiciting Christians being burned alive under the scrutiny of Nero and his fellow Romans. The painting, depicting human suffering and torment as it does, along with Semiradsky's inscription on the frame—"And a light burns in the darkness but the darkness does not overcome it"—would logically have had a great effect on someone as sensitive as Garshin.

And indeed his article consists less of a discussion of the work's artistic merit (other than a comment on Semiradsky's unimpeachable technique) than of a portrayal of the physical features of persecutors and persecuted. Thus he sees Nero as "puffy, dark, satiated, bored. . . . In Penelope's face nothing is visible except sensuousness" (323). In like manner, Garshin describes the physical traits of an old man, a gladiator, a young woman, and several Christians. He deviates from describing the physical aspects of the faces in the painting only to discuss briefly Semiradsky's errant use of light, which, he suggests, is the work's only failing. Garshin would use many of the techniques of literary Impressionism in his fiction: one such technique is the careful use of light and illumination to provide tone and contrast. Therefore it is appropriate that he pointed up Semiradsky's inability to use light and shadow, color and tone:

Semiradsky chose for his painting a most difficult time—early dusk. The sun has just gone down: the sunset, as always in the south, is unassuming and pale, the darkness comes quickly. The whole painting, all the figures, all the marble and ornamentation should be covered with the gray tones of the approaching darkness; the gold should not shine brightly, the draperies should not *shout* with their bright tones. (329)[1]

In "Konkurs na postoiannoi vystavke khudozhestvennykh proizvedenii" (The Competition at the Permanent Art Exhibition), the author delves a little more deeply into the motivation and background of the artist. He notes, for example, that by and large Russian artists are more successful with landscapes than with genre-paintings, attributing this to their divorce from their native soil, from true Russian life. Unable to deal with the drama of real life, the artists resort to the landscapes which dominated the competition. Garshin sees in competition itself an obstacle to the best in art, since the artist's goal becomes a prize, and a financial one at that. Garshin distinguishes these individuals from those artist-poets who in their creations are able continually to relive the moment of inspiration. When dealing with nature, for example, such artists paint not for effect, but to show their love and, even more important, their respect for nature.

The last of Garshin's 1877 articles was "Imperatorskaia akademiia khudozhestv za 1876–1877 uchebnyi god" (The Imperial Academy of Art for the 1876–1877 Academic Year). As in his previous articles, he is critical of the exhibition he is reporting on: indeed his first paragraph expresses his foreboding over the future of Russian art. He sees the Academy itself as a hindrance to the development of a creative school of Russian art, and in fact, the Academy's practice of prescribing subjects certainly did little to foster artistic creativity.

Garshin comments, for example, on the fact that the Academy may award an artist third place instead of first or second because he has failed to paint on the assigned theme. The theme in this particular example is "Golgotha": though the artist has painted Christ, he has depicted him prior to the crucifixion. Garshin rightly complains that not only must the artist paint on command, but he must intuit the detailed expectations of such a command.

After a hiatus of three years, Garshin published two articles in 1880: "Khudozhestvennaia vystavka v Peterburge" (An Artistic Exhibition in St. Petersburg) and "Vystavka v pomeshchenii 'Obshchestva pooshchreniia khudozhnikov' " (An Exhibition on the Premises of "The Society for the Encouragement of Artists").

The former article begins on an optimistic, impartial note as the author comments on the artistic promise of the new year. All the better artists of both camps—the Wanderers and the Society of Art Exhibitions—are working on new creations and promise to produce a varied crop of worthwhile works. Garshin then devotes a large part of the article to cataloging the more famous artists and the paintings on which each is working.

A smaller part of the article consists of a discourse on "tendencies" as philosophically defined by both camps. However, he says, this is not the determining factor in selecting works for exhibition: "The content of the latest exhibitions eloquently attests to the fact that each society is very little concerned about any kind of 'tendency,' but they accept for exhibition works of every conceivable type so long as they are not too poorly executed" (344–45). Garshin, who had published his most tendentious work, "Khudozhniki" (The Artists), shortly before this article appeared, obviously faults the groups for departing from the basic idea of socially useful art.

In his concluding paragraph Garshin calls for unity between the two artistic camps, arguing that the Wanderers and the Society of Art Exhibitions are not really that divergent in their ideas and ideals, but that personal animosities have caused them to become rivals. Russian art would be better served, he suggests, if the two groups combined their strengths and resources instead of indulging in senseless and debilitating acrimony.

Garshin begins "An Exhibition on the Premises of the 'Society for the Encouragement of Artists' " by complaining that the exhibit consists of three separate parts and the viewer is forced to pay separately for each. Garshin feels this is a burden primarily on the young, on whom art has the most wholesome effect (unfortunately he does not develop this rather interesting concept any further). He does enlighten the reader as to the character of the exhibition by discussing appropriateness of subject matter (a tortured child), proportion (he mentions a painting in which a peasant is drawn to such a large scale that his horse resembles a dog), and artistic technique (an artist whose works are distinguised "by the delicate fluency of his brushstrokes" [349]).

Garshin's final and longest article, "Zametki o khudozhestvennykh vystavkakh" (Notes on Art Exhibitions), appeared in 1887 in *Severny vestnik* (Northern Gazette). It begins with a general discussion of whether an art critic who himself is not a painter can accurately evaluate the artistic creations of others. In discussing the role of the critic, Garshin differentiates between the hack writer whose haphazard opinions on art appear in the daily newspapers, and true critics such as Vladimir Stasov, who, although himself not an artist, was greatly respected by the artistic community for his attachment to art and his perceptive observations on it.

We the viewers are also critics, Garshin suggests, though we tend to view a work of art in terms of whether it appears to be good or bad from the standpoint of technique. An artist, however, knows very well whether his technique is strong or weak, and therefore expects something else from the viewer. He wants to peer into the soul of the viewer, to grasp the impression made by his work; he wants to affect "the crowd," for an artist does not paint for another artist, but for those who are not artists and for himself. Garshin, propounding a rather commonplace notion, argues that the artist stands out from the crowd because he sees more clearly than the masses and transmits his visions to them. Garshin then goes on to discuss works by two such artists, Vasily Polenov and Vasily Surikov. Polenov's biblical painting (taken from the eighth chapter of John) deals with the woman taken in adultery. The crowd inquires of Jesus whether to follow Moses' commandment that such a woman be stoned, to which Jesus replies that whoever is without sin should cast the first stone. In discoursing on the painting, Garshin once again describes the participants in great detail, but provides little by way of perceptive analysis or emotional involvement. In minute detail he delineates those in the crowd who, as it happens, attract the viewer's gaze more than the adulteress or Jesus. He describes the woman, taking issue with critics who claim this "sinner" does not look the part. Garshin, who by this time had published his prostitute stories, maintains that anyone strolling the streets of St. Petersburg will discover similarly naive and childlike faces on the young "sinners" of the city.

Only in speaking of Jesus does Garshin discard physical description to offer his own personal comments. He argues that Jesus does not dominate the painting, for He has not yet begun to act. His acts— dispersing the mob, forgiving the woman—come later. It is the crowd pushing the woman forward which is at the center of the painting: the crowd is the active force seeking blood, both the woman's and Jesus'.

The second work, *The Boyarinya Morozova*, Vasily Surikov's most famous painting, also contains a crowd and a woman accused of a crime. An Old Believer is being taken to prison through the streets of medieval Moscow in an open cart. In contrast to Polenov's humble criminal, Morozova is proud and defiant as she raises her shackled hands to give the Old Believer a two-fingered sign. In his discussion of the work, Garshin provides some historical background on Morozova the person, as well as presenting information on the customs and traditions of her age (he even footnotes two works he used for reference).

Garshin stands in awe of Surikov's painting. He praises both the depiction of Morozova, which continues to affect the viewer long after he has finished studying the painting, and Surikov's treatment of the crowd, whose breath, the author asserts, seems to brush the viewer's very face. Still, the author devotes most of his article to a physical description of the crowd, which contains people sympathetic, hostile, or totally indifferent to the martyr.

Garshin's art criticism matured with time. Thus in an article of 1877 he naively denounces a painting of a feast because the artist had only painted two bottles on the table, exclaiming, "What kind of feast is possible when, for twenty people, only two bottles are provided" (341). But by the time he published his last article on art, in 1887, he had developed a more sophisticated artistic point of view, as, for instance, when he wrote that the critic should "evaluate not the artist, nor his painting, but our impressions of his work, that very milk upon which we feed" (353–54).

By and large, however, Garshin is descriptive rather than analytical in his criticism. He seldom discusses the subtle, the profound, the symbolic, seldom deals with the emotional, inner forces of art. His inability to go beyond the level of pure description may be attributed to a variety of causes. First, Garshin lacked experience with art, as he published most of his art criticism (four articles at the age of twenty-two) before he had written the bulk of his fiction. Second, he was tied to the Wanderers, who believed theme should dominate over form. The Wanderers were not against arousing emotion through art—that was in fact a cornerstone of their beliefs— but they wanted a painting or sculpture to stimulate direct and straightforward reactions. They therefore took little interest in halftones, subtle lines, or ambigious themes. Third, and most important, Garshin simply lacked the ability to analyze art on any but the most superficial level. His art criticism, like his poetry, has relatively little artistic merit and sheds little light on his personal view of art and creativity. That he was a talented writer is evident from his prose fiction; that he was a hack critic, to use his own terminology, is evident from his art criticism.

II *"An Occurrence"* (1878)

The theme of the artist and the prostitute interested Garshin throughout his literary career. At first he treated the topic as two separate themes—"An Occurrence" centers on a prostitute; "The Artists," as its title makes clear, is devoted to art. Near the end of

his life, though, he merged the two themes in his longest work,
"Nadezhda Nikolaevna," the story of an artist's involvement with
a prostitute.

"An Occurrence" is largely the story of a prostitute, Nadezhda
Nikolaevna, who relates the details of her encounter with a customer, Ivan Ivanovich. The latter, after visiting her once, falls in
love with her and attempts to "save" her. Nadezhda refuses his help
and Ivan, realizing his attempts have come to nothing, shoots himself.

A plot summary fails to do justice to this particular story, for it
is not the events in it which are important (as they are in the fairy
tales), but the heroine's perception of those events. Since the story
is narrated almost entirely by Nadezhda, we are privy both to her
actions and to the psychological effects of her actions.

As in "Four Days," the events related in the work have already
taken place, and the narrator is recalling an incident from the past.
We quickly learn some details of Nadezhda's past, her present, her
future: her seduction at seventeen by a dandy, her hostility toward
"good society," her present loneliness, her misanthropy ("How
should I think that there are good people in the world when out
of the scores whom I know, there is not one whom I could not
hate?" [17]), her thoughts of eventually ending her life by leaping
into a canal.

This introduction then leads Nadezhda back to an event of two
years before, when Ivan Ivanovich, a man of twenty-five, visited
her once and fell in love with her. The originality of Garshin's story
from this point on lies in his treatment of his prostitute-heroine as
a strong-willed, defiant character, in sharp contrast, for example,
to Dostoevsky's meek, submissive, "good" prostitutes. Nadezhda
realizes that Ivan Ivanovich offers her an escape from her present
life: "I need only hint at it and I will become a legal wife" (20).

Yet Nadezhda does not take this path, for she feels that marriage
to Ivan "will be the same sale. Lord no, it will be even worse!" (25).
And it will be worse, for Ivan will always have the power to remind
her of what she was: "It seems to me this man, if I give him control
over me, will torment me with one remembrance" (25). Rather than
risk losing her independence, she refuses Ivan's offer, thereby preserving her own personality and destroying Ivan Ivanovich's.

In his stories dealing with the artist and/or the prostitute, Garshin
always acquaints the reader with both sides represented in each

story. Thus he interrupts Nadezhda's narrative with Ivan's, utilizing either a first-person narrative or an epistolary form. In this way we understand the effect his entanglement with Nadezhda has on him: his mental and physical state deteriorates to the point where he seems to relish his suffering. This emerges in a very Dostoevskian scene where Ivan, having followed Nadezhda and a customer to her apartment, sits in a loft staring at the white curtains of her room while his face and feet freeze.

Afraid of Nadezhda when sober, Ivan resorts to drink in order to bolster his courage. Instead of winning her over, however, his drunken visits arouse her pity. At times she vacillates over her decision to marry him, but always at the back of her mind is her certainty that at some point in the future he will reject her. "If I were to marry him?" she asks. "A new life, new hopes. . . . Isn't it possible that the feeling of pity I now feel for him will change to love? Oh, no! Now he is ready to lick my hand, but then . . . he will trample me underfoot and say: 'Ah! You still oppose me, contemptible creature! You despised me!' " (26).

The ever present conviction that, if she lets down her guard, if she gives in, if she trusts Ivan, she will suffer for it later, causes her to remain firm in her decision to decline his proposal. She resolves instead to continue her present life for a few more years and then end it in suicide, the ultimate escape.

Ivan has one final encounter with Nadezhda in his room. As she knocks, she hears a drawer rapidly being closed, but thinks nothing of it. Ivan takes his final leave of her, telling her he is departing on a journey.[2] As she descends the steps, she realizes that he has a revolver in his drawer and that he is going to shoot himself. She races back to his room, but is too late: a shot rings out as she touches the doorknob. She faints and the story ends.

Thanks to the story's inverted structure—the beginning occurs two years after the ending—we can reassess the effect Ivan had on Nadezhda. The fact that Nadezhda has indeed been affected by him is made clear in several ways. Thus she exclaims: "Lord, stop him! Lord, leave him for me!" (31); she resorts to drink to forget "those oppressive thoughts" (15); she claims, in the later story "Nadezhda Nikolaevna," that she killed him.

Garshin's comment on the story clearly demonstrates what interested him in creating it. In a letter to his mother, he declared that *Otechestvennye zapiski* probably would not publish the story because "it does not at all pertain to war, to social, political, or to other questions. Simply the torments of two broken souls. . . . "

III *"Nadezhda Nikolaevna"* (1885)

Though not published until 1885, "Nadezhda Nikolaevna" was actually begun before "An Occurrence." Garshin started it in 1878 and worked on it sporadically over the next seven years.[4]

If "An Occurrence" is the story of "two broken souls," then "Nadezhda Nikolaevna" is the story of three broken souls—Nadezhda, Lopatin, and Bessonov. Lopatin, an artist, is unable to complete a portrait of Charlotte Corday because he cannot find a suitable model. An acquaintance, Bessonov, tells Lopatin he knows the perfect model, but refuses to introduce her to him. Lopatin's friend, the hunchback Gelfreykh, eventually introduces Lopatin to the "perfect model": the prostitute Nadezhda. Lopatin resumes work on his portrait with Nadezhda posing as Charlotte Corday. Nadezhda is as meek and unassuming as Lopatin and the two fall in love, the very thing Bessonov had feared. Rather than release Nadezhda, whom he loved and might have saved from her life of prostitution, he now kills her. In an attempt to save her, Lopatin hurls a spear at Bessonov at the very moment Bessonov raises his revolver. Lopatin kills Bessonov just as he kills Nadezhda. Lopatin alone survives to ponder his lost love.

Structually "Nadezhda Nikolaevna" is very similar to "An Occurrence": a primary narrator recalls a tragic event from the past which still disturbs him; through the use of a diary, Garshin enables us to view events through the eyes of a secondary narrator; in both works death prevents the fulfillment of happiness; both works have inverted chronological structure; both have a prostitute, Nadezhda Nikolaevna, as their lead female character.

Though the presence of Nadezhda links the two prostitute stories, the use of paintings as focal points connects "Nadezhda Nikolaevna" with "The Artists." The primary painting in the former story is Lopatin's painting of Charlotte Corday, which serves as the principal connection between Lopatin and Bessonov. The possibility of taking Charlotte Corday as the subject for a painting is initially raised in an argument between the two. Bessonov believes that Lopatin should not even consider such a topic:

One must have it in one's blood. One must be a descendant of those people who lived with Marat and Charlotte Corday, and that whole time period. But what are you? The softest Russian intellectual, dull, weak! One must be capable of the same act. But you? Are you able, if necessary, to throw away your brushes and, figuratively speaking, seize the dagger? You know for you this is equivalent to a trip to Jupiter" (231).

Lopatin counters by asking Bessonov if it were necessary for Rafael to become the Blessed Virgin in order to paint "The Madonna." Though Garshin poses the question rhetorically, it is answered not with philosophical arguments but through the actions of the characters involved.

Karl Kramer, an American literary scholar, is only partially correct in suggesting that "the fact that Lopatin finally kills Bessonov underscores the irony of the question,"[5] where the question has to do with whether or not Lopatin is able to "seize the dagger." There is certainly an irony here, but it is double-edged. The weak and passive Lopatin does rise up, like Charlotte Corday, to take the life of a fellow human. This certainly refutes Bessonov's assertion that the subject of a murderer such as Charlotte Corday is inappropriate for an intellectual like Lopatin. Yet ultimately he is really (much like Raskolnikov in Dostoevsky's *Crime and Punishment*) unable to bear the thought that he has murdered. Even though absolved of guilt—that is, legal culpability—by his peers, Lopatin is nevertheless unable to live with his deed and suffers from psychological torment: "But for the human conscience there are no written laws, no doctrine of irresponsibility, and I am undergoing punishment for my crime. . . . Soon God will forgive me" (288).

So on the physical level Bessonov is wrong about the painting and Lopatin, so much so that his misreading of Lopatin's nature causes his, Bessonov's, death. On the metaphysical level, however, Bessonov is correct. Lopatin is able to "seize the dagger," but unlike Charlotte Corday he cannot live with his act.

The function of the painting in the story, like the irony discussed above, is dichotomous. From the Charlotte Corday point of view, it presents the theoretical, artistic side of the Lopatin-Bessonov conflict, in which the author contrasts their different viewpoints on the nature of art. From the Nadezhda Nikolaevna point of view, the dichotomy manifests itself in the physical, emotional, human side of the confrontation.

Although Charlotte Corday and Nadezhda Nikolaevna represent

different foci of this primary symbol, they are inextricably bound
to each other in the minds of the three male characters—Bessonov,
Gelfreykh, Lopatin—who have contact with the prostitute.
Bessonov is the first to link the two, for he knows she will be the
perfect model for the painting. Gelfreykh comes to the same conclusion; moreover, he ensures that Lopatin does meet her. In point-
ing her out to him he exclaims, "This is she, your Charlotte Corday"
(240). And Lopatin equates the two in his mind on many occasions,
though perhaps most strongly when she first sits for him: "In front
of me stood my painting" (247).

By presenting the symbol now as a single focus, now as two
separate foci, Garshin multiplies and complicates the levels of interaction between Bessonov and Lopatin so that, as their perceptions of the major symbol change, so too do their perceptions of
each other.

Lopatin mentions that his idea of painting Charlotte Corday
comes in part from Lamartine's writings about her. Alphonse Marie
Louis de Lamartine (1790–1869), a prolific and popular French poet,
was also an influential statesman and historian whose greatest prose
work, *Histoire des Girondins*, is the source of Lopatin's information
on Charlotte Corday. Among his other scholarly endeavors, Lamartine also published a history of Russia. The similarity between
Garshin's work and Lamartine's, however, lies primarily within the
structural rather than the thematic realm. Both use the central
figure of a woman as the object of two men's attention. In addition
to equating Nadezhda with Charlotte, Garshin matches Lopatin to
Hauer, who painted Charlotte, and Bessonov to Fauchet, who loved
without being loved. Even Gelfreykh finds a counterpart in Lamartine's Adam Lux.[6]

Aside from the similar structural arrangement of characters and
the central figure of Charlotte Corday, there are few links between
Lamartine and Garshin. As a matter of fact, Garshin's only comment
on Lamartine occurs in a letter to Fausek, in which he complains
that he is a "horrible chatterbox."[7] Ironically Garshin, usually the
epitome of brevity and precision in his prose, discards these traits
in this story, by far his longest, and instead rambles, sometimes
quite needlessly, à la Lamartine.

As "Nadezhda Nikolaevna" progresses, Bessonov and Lopatin vie
for the title character. In so doing, each reveals various facets of his

personality, which changes as a consequence of her influence. In
the end each has exchanged positions with the other. Lopatin is
placed in the role which Bessonov had occupied three years previously, that of a savior to Nadezhda. For three years Bessonov had
refused to acknowledge that he had loved her or that she was capable
of being saved. He refuses to acknowledge that he loves her even
when Lopatin confronts him with such a possibility.

As Bessonov watches Lopatin assume the role of Nadezhda's savior, he is driven to the breaking point. He reaches that point when,
failing to win Nadezhda's love, be becomes completely debilitated
and forfeits his position of dominance.

Conversely, Lopatin, who initially appears to be a weak character,
grows in prominence as his association with Nadezhda leads him
to assume a dominant role. As he grows in stature, he earns the
respect not only of Nadezhda, but of the male characters too. Bessonov, Gelfreykh, and Grum-Skzhebitsky, the Polish landlord, all
at some point in the story declare themselves envious of Lopatin.

Nadezhda affects the two men on the most physical of levels.
Though each is an intellectual, an educated member of society,
neither can face the other in a reasonable, rational manner. As the
two have increasingly greater contact with her, their relationship
with each other deteriorates. Garshin emphasizes Nadezhda's effect
on the passions of the two by showing each in relation to a different
female. Bessonov, we learn from Lopatin, is a devoted son; Lopatin
is engaged to Sonya. This latter relationship is described in great
depth and detail, in a way which emphasizes the changes Lopatin
undergoes because of Nadezhda. Sonya is a stylized, totally good,
totally outgoing person akin to Dostoevsky's Sonya Mermeladova.
She is always ready to soothe and succor Lopatin, and even to
relinquish her right to him.

In contrast to this relationship, Lopatin's love for Nadezhda—a
prostitute and a model for an assassin—reveals a great deal about
his own character and stresses the transformation he undergoes. In
the beginning we feel he is much like Sonya; in the end we alter
our opinion. Bessonov also undergoes an alteration in character,
but the important point here is the source of the change. As the
two male characters shift, as their positions rotate, they do so around
the female focus represented by Nadezhda Nikolaevna–Charlotte
Corday.

IV *"The Artists"* (1879)

The central image in this work is also a painting, *Glukhar* (The Human Anvil).[8] By refracting the disparate views of two artists, Dedov and Ryabinin, through the prism of the painting, Garshin presents their views on art, and, concomitantly, of each other.

The story consists of eleven brief chapters. Each chapter has a first-person narrator—Dedov in the odd-numbered, Ryabinin in the even-numbered chapters—who presents his perceptions of the events which unfold. Dedov, after receiving a small inheritance, gives up his work in a factory to devote his life to art. He is excited by art, in contrast to his friend Ryabinin, for whom art has become boring and creativity is passé. He perceives a deeper meaning in art and is tormented by the question "why?" One day while walking with Dedov, Ryabinin is introduced to a world he hadn't previously known: the factory world Dedov has left. In the factory Ryabinin finds a new subject, the human anvil. The human anvil is so called because his job consists of crawling into a boiler and grasping a rivet with pincers, pressing against the rivet with his whole body while someone outside the boiler hammers the rivet until he has beaten a head on it. Ryabinin crawls into a boiler to watch the process firsthand and crawls out obsessed with the idea of painting the human anvil. Ryabinin succeeds in completing his painting, but the price is great: for days he is in a state of delirium; upon recovering, he abandons art altogether and decides to become a teacher.

The views of the two artists on art are, at first glance, diametrically opposed. Dedov sees painting as limited exclusively to the realm of nature. Art is gentle; art is satisfying. To him art is a means to a financial end: "While you're working on a painting—you're an artist, a creator," he says. "Once it is finished—you're a huckster" (79). He respects and admires Ryabinin's "devilishly talented nature" (78), but he not only cannot accept the subjects Ryabinin chooses for his paintings, he severely criticizes him for selecting them.

Art for Dedov is an anodyne. He has forsaken another life, a harsh life in a factory, and he refuses to allow cruel memories from his past to interfere with his new, serene life centered around his paintings: "How many oppressive impressions in these factories, Ryabinin, if only you knew! I am so glad that I am through with them for ever" (80).

Dedov was anguished in his factory life; Ryabinin is tormented in his art. He cannot comprehend the cyclical nature of painting. He romanticizes the peaks of the emotion, the grief, and the joy expended by an artist, only to sell his creation in the end. As a result, art has begun to lose its appeal for him. Unable to answer the questions he himself raises ("Why do you do all this, where is it leading?" [77]), he temporarily quits painting, and the reader meets Ryabinin at a time when four months have passed since the sale of his last work.

Before confronting Ryabinin and Dedov with *The Human Anvil* as a focus for each man's views on art, Garshin first presents the artist in connection with different works. Their comments on these works precede their opinions of *The Human Anvil.*

Dedov, while boating on a river—that is, in the nature setting he esteems so highly and which inspires him so much—paints the oarsman rowing his boat. His love for the pure mechanics of his craft is apparent: "With an especially joyous feeling, I mixed the paints" (74). Though the setting is natural, the painting is not: the rower, so unpretentious and lively when actually rowing, becomes affected when forced to pose. In the former instance, "he worked the oars without pause" (74); in the latter he "soon began to tire; his daring, expressive face was replaced by one which was dull and boring. He began to yawn" (74). Dedov, however, fails to see the artificiality of the situation and becomes vexed with the rower when he can no longer sit still.

In this scene Garshin emphasizes two aspects of Dedov's outlook on art: the financial and the technical. When the rower asks Dedov what the painting is for, he replies: "I didn't begin to give him a lecture on the significance of art, but merely said that for these paintings people pay good money, a thousand rubles, two thousand and more" (75). From the opening pages, when he speaks of his aunt's inheritance, to the discussions of the wealthy artist "K" and his lucrative career, to the end, when he receives his stipend to go abroad, Dedov is overly concerned with money. Moreover, in each instance this money is in some way connected to his art.

In addition to money, Dedov is enthralled with artistic technique, especially the use of color. His comment when he finishes the rower is that it came out fine, especially "those burning tones of calico red illuminated by the setting sun" (75).

Ryabinin paints his picture in the academy, where the setting is quite different from Dedov and the oarsman. His model Taras, a professional, is more alive, almost more natural, when posing than when resting between sittings, at which time "the model turned into an ordinary, naked old man" (75). Of course Ryabinin, in contrast to Dedov, is aware of the artificiality of this painting. He realizes that the model and the setting are sham, that his work lacks value, that it is without any feeling. Rather than creating, he is simply reproducing something. This is emphasized by his closing comment on his painting: "Taras stood out on the canvas, as though alive" (77).

Up to this point, the reader has perceived each artist and his relation to art separately. When *The Human Anvil* is introduced, however, Garshin interweaves the conflicting views of the two artists to show causes and effects by obverting the symbol now on one, now on the other. The painting connects the artists on several planes. Its primary function is to provide a platform for their divergent philosophies of art, thereby contrasting the two as artists, but it also sets off the two as men and illustrates how each views his fellow man. The symbol is, in addition, a connector on a temporal plane. *The Human Anvil* serves to tie Dedov's past to Ryabinin's future: what the former has given up—i.e., his factory life—becomes for the latter his fate.

Although it is Ryabinin who communicates his intention of painting *The Human Anvil* to the reader—"I will paint him" (81), he says—it is Dedov who describes how Ryabinin first becomes acquainted with the subject. He tells, for example, how Ryabinin crawls out of the boiler "pale and disturbed" *(blednyi i rasstroennyi).*[9] While discussing Ryabinin and *The Human Anvil,* Dedov is, of course, prejudiced by his own thoughts and feelings, as is Ryabinin, but by alternating each artist's diary entry, Garshin permits the reader to judge each prejudice in light of its counterpart.

The confrontation the painting provokes centers mainly on the subject matter and the functions of art. Dedov grants that paintings such as Ilya Repin's *The Barge Haulers* and, we might add, Nikolay Yaroshenko's *The Stoker,* which served as a model for Garshin, "are painted excellently, there is no argument there; but that is all" (81).

In utter opposition to Ryabinin's work, Dedov speaks of his own creation, *A May Morning,* which he characterizes as "serene" *(tixoe).* He feels his work is successful and worthwhile, for "it disposes a man to a quiet, gentle pensiveness; it soothes the soul" (82), while Ryabinin's lacks "beauty, harmony, refinement" (81). Dedov's philosophy of art is expressed by the author in one sentence: "And doesn't art exist for the reproduction of the refined in nature?" (81). This is far removed from Ryabinin's conception of art. Rather than being pacified by his artistic creation, he is incited by it: "The work torments me tremendously although it is going well. Rather one should say not *although*, but *the more so* that it is going well. The closer it moves towards its completion, the more horrible that which I have painted appears to me" (82).[10]

He refers to his work, not as a painting, not as a creation, but as a "festering illness." Ryabinin, whose main concern with a work of art is that it should influence the viewer, succeeds in painting such a work, but the influence it has on Ryabinin is negative: he first falls ill and then gives up painting altogether. Nevertheless, he wants *The Human Anvil* to affect others as it has affected him. He addresses his painting as if it were a person: "Strike them in the chest, deprive them of sleep, stand before their eyes like a specter. Destroy their serenity as you have destroyed mine" (83).

The reader never really learns whether the painting has the desired effect. Ryabinin speculates on the reactions his work will evoke, but in the end we are told only that "the painting was sold and carted off to Moscow" (85). In contrast, Dedov's painting does produce the desired result: he wins the gold medal and the opportunity to study abroad.

As "The Artists" develops, it seem Ryabinin is treated more and more ironically. His painting is a significant accomplishment, and he falls ill from his endeavors; he receives money for the work, but dissipates all that he earned in a night of carousing; his creation forces him to take a new approach to life, so he decides to become a teacher; but even here, the author confides to the reader, "Ryabinin really did not succeed" (91).

Eventually Dedov succeeds and Ryabinin fails, but Garshin does not imply that Dedov's views on art are therefore any more valid than Ryabinin's. As in "Vstrecha" (The Meeting), the ending, instead of providing unequivocal answers, confronts the reader with unanswerable questions. And, as with "The Meeting," the author's attitude itself is somewhat ambivalent.

Garshin's sympathies are for the most part with Ryabinin, but this does not mean that he opposes Dedov entirely. Dedov is not a negative stick figure created by Garshin solely with unattractive features. The portrayal of his character is complex. Likewise, Ryabinin does not exhibit totally positive traits. These are intricate characters who cannot easily be pigeon-holed as right or wrong, good or evil, etc. The painting symbolizes the contrasting artistic views of Dedov and Ryabinin, but it also is a focal point of the changes the two undergo as men. *The Human Anvil* complicates Ryabinin's character, making him a more tragic figure, while concurrently Dedov's character softens. Because of the painting's effect on Ryabinin, Dedov expresses genuine concern and pity for his friend as a man, even though he cannot commiserate with him as an artist. The artistic and other distinctions, so apparent and pronounced in the beginning, now blur.

Ultimately neither view of art triumphs, because neither artist espouses a comprehensively valid theory of art which coincides with the author's. In discussing the ambiguity inherent in the story, Karl Kramer makes the following pointed observations:

Apparently, we are looking at the contrasting views of two artists: Dedov, an engineer who . . . decides to devote himself to art, which he fondly believes is a world unto itself. Ryabinin, a fellow painter, strives to depict social reality. . . . These outlines appear clearly in the story, and yet neither artist speaks authoritatively for his point of view. Indeed, each contradicts the conventional role into which he might seem to have been cast.[11]

Thus Dedov, who at times deviates from the doctrine of art for art's sake, is in no way the embodiment of pure art. On the one hand, as Kramer says, he is "obviously echoing the impressionist painters in his character's plea for a revolution in color, while on the other hand he supports the realist's cause in demanding a more accurate reflection of reality in art."[12] Ryabinin, too, deviates from his role as social artist. His pronouncement that in a painting an artist creates a new world independent of external morality is far removed from the theory that an artist should promote social good through art.

"Thus," Karl Kramer writes, "the conclusion of the story is indeterminate, and the neat contrast with which it seemed to be concerned has given way to a complex and unsolvable dillemma."[13] This dilemma is concentrated on the central symbol of the painting; this is its function in the story. Some of Garshin's contemporaries believed that the real hero of the story was ultimately *The Human Anvil* itself, but this exaggerates its role.[14] *The Human Anvil* is a device important for the light it sheds on, and the reactions it evokes from, the two artists. The painting, like the aquarium in "The Meeting," is a symbol necessary for the posing of questions, and in both works it is the presentation of the problem, not its resolution, which concerns the author. Actually, this statement is true of most of Garshin's stories. His works are not a series of answers, but a series of questions.

V Social Questions

The stories dealing with art and prostitutes are not among Garshin's best; they fall short of the military tales and "The Red Flower."

"An Occurrence," "Nadezhda Nikolaevna," and "The Artists" are greatly weakened by their tendentiousness and by overdramatization. The conclusions of these stories—Nadezhda putting her hand on the doorknob at the very instant Ivan Ivanovich shoots himself, or Lopatin hurling the spear at the very moment that Bessonov shoots Nadezhda, or Dedov's chance encounter with Ryabinin on the day the former is to go abroad—are contrived and melodramatic actions which detract from their artistry.

Likewise the narrative techniques used in the art/prostitute stories suffer by comparison with the military tales. In the former Garshin attempts to introduce the reader to the inner worlds of both hero and foil by the use of alternating narratives, usually in the form of a diary; but by trying to present the inner viewpoints of persons on both sides of the artistic, moral, philosophical, or social questions he considers, he weakens his stories. The dual diaries seem contrived.

The military stories, on the other hand, are realistic works related by a believable first-person narrator. Based as they are on the author's own experiences, and if anything underplayed, they far surpass the artist/prostitute stories in craft and verisimilitude.

Of course, since he wrote at a time when social themes were often considered more important than artistic merit, it is not surprising that Garshin should have succumbed to this temptation. Viewed in his time as a social writer, and in fact genuinely concerned with the issues of his day, he did occasionally feel the need to express his concern through his literature. As a result some of his stories—those discussed in this chapter—are tendentious and dated.

In addition to the didactic and melodramatic tones which lower the artistry of these works, they are further weakened by poor character portrayal, especially in the case of the secondary characters. The characters who parade before the reader—the sniveling Ivan Ivanovich, the angelic Sonya, the fawning Polish landlord, the loyal hunchback—strain his credulity. Add to this the maudlin scenes, the exhortations and pontifications of the main characters, the unbelievable endings, and the final result falls far short of great literature.

In specifically dealing with art, i.e., in his articles and stories on the subject, Garshin seemed unable to resist the temptation to use art as a directly didactic instrument. In his fairy tales the tendentious approach is appropriate and enjoyable; in his "art" works, the result is tedious. Fortunately, when Garshin treated art not as a subject, but as an approach or a technique, as in his military stories and "The Red Flower," he produced artistic literature of a high order. His fame deservedly rests on these latter works.

CHAPTER 5

The Tales of Insanity

I *"A Night"* (1880)

" A Night," one of Garshin's poorer works, describes the last
hours in the life of a disillusioned young man who has decided
to commit suicide. As he prepares to do away with himself, recurrent
memories of childhood overwhelm him so that his final act is repeatedly delayed. Finally he realizes that "it is necessary 'to reject'
oneself, to kill one's 'I' " (116), at which point he experiences a
tremendous surge of emotion. In the morning he is found dead with
a serene expression on his face.

"A Night" is too overdone to be a successful analysis of the last
hours of a deranged individual. The modern reader is not enthralled
by Garshin's hackneyed, pointedly direct treatment of his theme,
although among Garshin's contemporaries, especially advocates of
literature as social criticism, the story was successful. Mikhail Saltykov-Shchedrin, the famous writer and editor of *Otechestvennye
zapiski*, for example, notified Garshin, who had sent him the manuscript, that, "having read your story, I find it to be very good and
I intend to include it in the March issue."[1]

The story opens with a watch ticking on a table top, reminding
the protagonist, Aleksey Petrovich, of the inexorable passing of
time. He feels that all he has pursued in life has been unreal and
that the only reality is time. Traveling back in time through his
memories, Aleksey Petrovich finds no comfort in the past "because
all is falsehood, all is deception. And I lied and deceived myself"
(102). At this point the narrator intervenes with a clarification: "He
didn't notice that in classifying his whole life a deception and in
sullying himself, he was, at that moment, telling a lie—the worst
lie in the world—a lie to oneself. For the fact of the matter was he
did not really have such a low opinion of himself" (102).

Repeatedly in the story reality is contrasted with Aleksey's perception of it. As a literary technique this could have been used very effectively if Garshin had maintained the two voices, i.e., the narrator's and the protagonist's. Instead, he introduces another three voices speaking in Aleksey's soul. The voices serve little purpose and become a jarring affectation.

In the first chapter of "A Night" we learn that Aleksey Petrovich has been sitting at his desk from eight o'clock at night till three o'clock in the morning, contemplating suicide. The second chapter, in a chronological reversal, describes the protagonist's trip at seven o'clock in the evening to a friend's home to steal his pistol, which is obviously to be the instrument of his suicide. On his way there a coachman (a forerunner of Anton Chekhov's coachman in "Grief") talks about a young coachman, Ivan Sidorov, who committed suicide several days before.

Although this suicide is certainly meant to presage Aleksey's own, the stress in the story is not on the act itself, but on the memories of the past which the contemplated suicide evokes. The past was good, for "red was red then, and not the reflection of red rays" (111). He remembers his childhood, when he and his father were together; he recalls his Bible lessons, a peasant being slapped by a nobleman, and a little green book. He digs the book out of his desk and reads it until he finds a phrase which has always overwhelmed him: "Unless you become as children" (115).

This phrase becomes for him the key to a true, sincere life. "Do I know the meaning of these words? To become as a child! . . . It means not to place oneself first in all things, to tear out of one's heart this nasty little god, this monster with a huge belly, this disgusting I , which, like a worm, sucks one's soul and demands for itself ever new foods" (115).

The realization that he has discovered and grasped the meaning of life exerts a profound effect on him. As Garshin so melodramatically presents it:

He had never experienced such ecstasy neither from life's successes, nor from a woman's love. This ecstasy was born in the heart, burst from it gushing in a broad fiery wave, spreading to all his limbs. For an instant his numbed, unhappy being became feverish and enlivened. Thousands of bells solemnly resounded. The sun blindingly blazed up, illuminated the whole world and disappeared. (116–17)

The narrator then describes the room as it appeared the next morning. The loaded pistol is on the table; the corpse of Aleksey Petrovich is on the floor.

This ending raised questions of interpretation and occasioned no small degree of controversy among writers and critics. The modern reader is not troubled by the objects—a dead body and a loaded pistol—but Garshin's contemporaries could not reconcile the two.

Ivan Turgenev, for instance, in a postscript to a letter to Garshin from Bougival on September 3, 1882, asked: "Why did you say in the conclusion that there lay 'a human corpse'? He did not kill himself and it is not evident that he died from other causes. This lack of clarity produces an impression of bewilderment in the reader and should at all costs be avoided."[2]

It was the literary critic Nikolay Mikhailovsky, though, who committed the biggest literary *faux pas* by misreading the ending. Commenting on "A Night" in an article of December 1885, he wrote: "But this upheaval in Aleksey Petrovich did not last long: another little psychiatric tremor and he does away with himself."[3] Two months later, he was compelled to pen a new article in order to admit his error publicly:

I must return for a minute to Mister Garshin. He has brought to my attention a mistake I made in the last (December) "Diary" when I was speaking of his story "A Night." Giving the plot of this short story, I wrote that the hero decided on suicide, but a euphoric feeling temporarily caused him to hesitate; at the end of the story, however, he nevertheless shoots himself. V. M. Garshin explained to me that I had made a mistake: Aleksey Petrovich . . . did not shoot himself; he died from an overflowing of feeling. . . . The difference is great. I think, however, that I have not been the only one mistaken on this point and therefore I am making the greatest possible haste to correct my mistake."[4]

II "*The Red Flower*" (1883)

Writing to his friend Victor Fausek on July 9, 1883, Garshin, in speaking of several stories he was working on, notes that "one relates to the time of my stay at the Saburova Dacha: it's turning out somewhat fantastic, but the fact of the matter is it's strictly realistic."⁵ The "fantastic, realistic" work referred to is "The Red Flower," Garshin's most famous story.

The story relates the experiences of a nameless madman over a period of several days in an insane asylum. Soon after his arrival at the asylum, the madman sees red poppies growing in a flower bed and imagines that they contain all the evil in the world. By destroying the poppies he believes he can save the world from evil, though he realizes he himself may die in the attempt. In three separate "combats" the madman is victorious, but the effort proves fatal in the end.

Although the tale is a third-person narrative, much is related from the vantage point of the hero, who, since he is mad, sees objects and events differently from others: simple objects and actions acquire tremendous symbolic importance disproportionate to their real values. The flower, for example, becomes for the madman evil incarnate, and his struggle with this antagonist is the center of the story.

The madman is introduced to the reader directly through a detailed description by the omniscient narrator, and indirectly through the effect he has had on others. We see, for example, the clerk who smiles at his behavior, and the two escorts who have spent two exhausting days with him and who do not smile. In addition, we hear of the conductor and policeman who aided the escorts in encasing the madman in a straitjacket: they did not smile either during the ordeal with the madman.

Occasionally two points of view of the external reality of the asylum surface. Some objects (the red flowers, the other patients in the asylum) and relationships are seen subjectively, as the madman views them; others (the psychiatrist, the guards) are presented objectively. The asylum itself is described in a careful, detached, detailed manner, as though the narrator were thoroughly familiar with his surroundings. We feel we are on a guided tour as the narrator describes and explains which rooms are lined with mattresses and used for the violent patients, which halls are for dining or relaxing, which floors house men and which women. We learn the history of the asylum—that it was built for eighty inmates but now holds three hundred; we learn what the inmates do in winter as opposed to summer; we learn where each hallway goes, where each door leads, what each window looks out on.⁶

So in "The Red Flower" the reader witnesses a multi-dimensional presentation. The subjective alternates with the objective, the fantastic merges with the real. The narration is ultimately plausible because, though we enter into a madman's perceptions, we are exposed to them through a normal (and thus believable) narrator. The hero of this story is a madman, but even this point is questionable, for the author informs the reader that the protagonist's insane periods often alternate with times when he is "as though sane." His moments of lucidity appear and then fade away, to be replaced by delusions. By alternating these periods, Garshin makes his hero something more than a simple madman, his personality more complex, his actions less easily explained by mere lunacy. The more open to interpretation his actions are, the more complex his motives appear to the reader. This is especially true at the beginning of the story, before he becomes totally obsessed by the flower.

His contact with the plant gradually intensifies. His first impression of it is through the glass; his second encounter is in the garden when he compares the red cross on his cap to the flower and tries to pluck it; the third contact results in the actual picking of the plant. Again, by leaving intervals between these scenes Garshin further illuminates the madman's character, shows the oscillations of his thoughts, and demonstrates how his obsession with the flower eventually takes total hold of him. Since these contacts are crests of action in the work, Garshin is also able to increase or decrease tension, to speed up or slow down the action, by inserting other material between these episodes. (He used much the same technique in "Four Days" in the three descriptions of the corpse.) As the story progresses, the flower assumes an ever growing importance in the madman's mind. With each confrontation he becomes more and more affected until the lines of the imminent struggle between himself and the poppies are clearly defined. From this point on, he is consumed by a desire to destroy or be destroyed.

To be sure, the narrator offers a possible rationale for the madman's actions:

He knew that opium is made from poppies: perhaps this idea magnified in his mind to monstrous proportions, caused him to create that horrid fantastic specter. In his eyes the flower contained within itself all evil: it had soaked up all innocently spilled blood (that's why it was so red), all tears, all the bile of humanity. This was a secret, horrible creature the opposite of God—Ahriman in a modest and innocent aspect. (195)[7]

The symbolism then becomes clear. The flower is the personi-
fication of evil, the antithesis of God, i.e., Satan. The red of the
flowers recalls the dark red bath in which the madman underwent
his painful scrubbing which is "perhaps, Hell itself" (186). Opposing
this evil force is the hero, the madman. He considers himself a
warrior *(boets)*; his undertaking is an heroic exploit *(podvig)*. He
gives up his body, though not his soul, to St. George: "Holy martyr
St. George. Into your hands I give my body. But my soul—no, oh
no!" (186). The fact that "St. George governs wolves and serpents"[8]
is significant in view of the fact that in combat with one of the
flowers "the madman felt that evil was *coiling* up from the flower
in long *serpentlike* streams" (196).[9]

The hero also has other religious associations. He, like all the
inmates, as opposed to the guards, wears a hat with a cross, albeit
a red one. When on his way to his last battle with the flower, he
twice looks heavenward: "I am coming to You—he whispered, glancing at the sky" (199). "Wait," he said, glancing at the sky, "I will
soon be with You" (199).

On one level the struggle between good and evil in "The Red
Flower" is presented in spiritual, almost superhuman, terms. In his
combat with the flower, the hero exhibits cleverness, perseverance,
bravery, a nearly inhuman sacrifice of self to defeat his enemy. If
this larger-than-life role were maintained, if all events were viewed
in such strictly black and white, sharply delineated terms, this story
would more appropriately fit within the fairy-tale genre. Such is not
the case, however.

Interwoven into the story is a secondary level of meaning marking
off the madman as man, from the heroic warrior as superman. Garshin first describes his protagonist in the following manner: "He
looked terrible. . . . His bloodshot, dilated eyes (he had not slept
for ten days) burned with a fixed, intense sparkle: his lower lip
twitched with a nervous spasm; his matted, curly hair fell on his
forehead like a mane. He walked with rapid, heavy steps from one
corner of the office to the other" (184).

This is no portrait of a warrior; it is a picture of a man replete
with his insane weaknesses. Throughout the story Garshin emphasizes two aspects of the hero as man. On the one hand, he describes
the hero's physically deteriorating condition. The scenes with careful, day-to-day notations of weight loss, the hero's eating and sleeping habits, etc., serve to underscore his bodily weakness. On the

other hand, the author stresses his character's psychological foibles. His relentless pacing, his incoherent conversations with the other patients and the guards, reveal the true imbalance of the man. The total effect of this portrayal of madman as man, as opposed to madman as warrior, is to make his exploits seem even greater when compared to the reality of the situation. Thus, even though greatly weakened from lack of sleep and from loss of weight, he is able, after many hours' work, to free himself from his bonds. Even though supposedly crazy, he is capable of cleverly deceiving his guards, of shrewdly removing an iron bar in his cell window.

Both aspects of the madman are, of course, influenced by the flower, which is simultaneously attractive and repellent to him. The madman is fighting on the side of good against evil and, though he sees himself as a Christ figure, he gives up his body to the martyr St. George, but he refuses to cede his soul to him. While struggling in the bath, he calls out to God: "O You, who have already tormented me! I pray to You, deliver me" (186). This displays a degree of alienation from God if not animosity or fear toward Him. And just as he is not wholly attached to God, so he is not wholly detached from the red flower. His first inspection of the poppy evokes extreme malice, but his second contact with it begins with an almost alluring sensation which turns into a deadly attraction as the flower defends itself and tries to repel the madman.

A further tie between the madman and the flower is exemplified by the properties naturally inherent in the flower. The flower is a poppy, from which opium is derived. As mentioned above, this is one of the possibilities the narrator grants for the hero's association of evil with the plant. Another derivative of the poppy, though, is morphine, a medication taken by the madman himself! Significantly, it is not until the senior doctor mentions that "yesterday the morphine had no effect" (197) that the madman is at last successful in defeating the flower.

The tales of insanity draw, to be sure, on Garshin's own experiences with mental illness and his frequent incarcerations in asylums, but it would be a mistake to conclude that they are merely autobiographical sketches. They were read in that way by Garshin's contemporaries, but incorrectly so. They are works of literature and must be evaluated as such. Thus "A Night" is a poor story, for it lacks verisimilitude and is weak from the point of view of literary craft. The images used in the story are trite and hackneyed: a watch singing its notes, a watch to show the passing of time, a watch connected to the beat of the first-person narrator's heart. The protagonist's pronouncements also lack force and originality due to their overuse, as when he tells himself that "all is farce, all is deception" (102), or he opines that "there is only one reality—time" (100).

Perhaps the weakest aspect of "A Night" is, however, Garshin's inability to come to grips with narrative voice, or to put it more correctly, to come to grips with a narrative voice. The protagonist at times speaks directly in the first person, at times he carries on a dialogue with himself, at times other voices speak in his soul. The main body of the story is taken over by a third-person narrator who is largely omniscient, but who occasionally speaks with the first person narrator directly. [10]

Structurally the story lacks action, tension, and motivation. The flashbacks either impart information unnecessary to the story itself (such as how Aleksey comes by the gun) or describe mawkish scenes (such as those of his childhood) which are inconsistent and unmotivated in relation to the main story line.

"The Red Flower," on the other hand, is a well-constructed, well-thought-out artistic creation and has rightly endured as the story most often associated with the author's name. It is an original, effective, consistent treatment of insanity which undermines the theory that Garshin could write freely only with first-person narrators. [11]

In closing we should mention that "The Red Flower," though based on Garshin's experiences in an asylum, was written in 1883, the year he married Nadezhda Zolotilova, one of the happiest and most balanced periods of his life.

CHAPTER 6

Miscellaneous Tales

I "The Meeting" (1879)

"THE Meeting" relates a chance encounter between two former high-school friends, Vasily Petrovich and Nikolay Konstantinovich Kudryashov, in a provincial city. Vasily, arriving in the city to assume his first job, that of a schoolteacher, is overwhelmed by Kudryashov's material wealth—his excellent carriage, his richly adorned house, his inexhaustible supply of fine foods and wines. It turns out, to Vasily's amazement, that Kudryashov is involved in a conspiracy with several cohorts to cheat the government out of large sums of money annually on a dam-building project. Vasily, as naive as Kudryashov is callous, berates his friend for his lack of scruples, but in the end he is stunned into silence by Kudryashov's magnificent aquarium.

As the story opens Vasily is standing on the shore of a sea (presumably the Black Sea) looking out over a vast expanse of darkness broken only by a band of moonlight. From this vantage point he has an extremely limited perception of the area around him, seeing only what passes through the moonlit strip. Confined to this narrow physical plane, Vasily lapses into thought and surrenders himself to a series of sensations which he is experiencing for the first time:

> Vasily Petrovich, *who had never seen anything like this*, gazed pleasurably at the sea, the strip of light, the steamers and other ships, and joyfully, *for the first time in his life,* breathed the sea air. After having turned his back on the city at which *he had only arrived* today and in which he would have to live for many, many years, he stood for a long time taking pleasure in these sensations *which were so new to him.* (54)[1]

The horizons of this world expand as the motley crowds moving past compel Vasily to perceive the larger reality around him. One particular group, a crowd of students, especially attracts his attention, and he overhears snatches of a conversation.

"Don't believe him, Nina Petrovna! It's all lies. He's making it up!"
"But really, Nina Petrovna, I am not at all guilty!"
"Shevyrev, if you ever again imagine you can deceive me . . . " said the girl in a sedately restrained young voice. (55)

The conversation dealing with guilt and deception is no doubt intended to portend the events in the story proper.[2] Even the names are linked to the two main characters: Nina has the same patronymic as the hero, Vasily Petrovich; Shevyrev has a certain phonetic tie to Kudryashov apparent in the repetition of "r," "sh," and "ov."

The students perform a second function. Their presence draws Vasily into a reverie on his future life in this provincial town and his past dreams of academic distinction. He projects his dreams of greatness onto those students he will teach, and in a daydream filled with high-flown tropes he vicariously achieves respect and renown through them.

He, Vasily Petrovich, now a gray, old teacher, sits by himself in his modest apartment and is visited by his former students: one is a professor of such-and-such university who is famous "even in Europe"; another is a writer, a well-known novelist; the third is a statesman, also famous. And they all treat him with respect. "It was your good seed, sown in my soul when I was a youth which has made me what I am, Sir," says the statesman and with feeling he shakes the hand of his old teacher. (55)

The opening of "The Meeting" establishes a pattern of alternation between the real and the imagined. First, for example, we see the physical world in its fragmented parts through Vasily's eyes; then we see the world as he imagines and fantasizes it to be. The author then brings Vasily back to the real world from his daydreams of former students by recalling more mundane matters, viz., his present financial plight. These alternations allow Garshin to delineate Vasily's character. Though he is undeniably a dreamer and an idealist, there are other facets to his personality: he is affected by monetary considerations—he has squandered money all along the road to his new city, and he will be impressed by Kudryashov's opulent ambience. Though a dreamer, he is also a pragmatist—he and his fiancée have decided they need a thousand rubles before they can marry. Like Kudryashov, Vasily will also try to work through influential people, as is shown in the opening by his inspection "for the twentieth time" (56) of two letters addressed to local bosses.

Along with these letters Vasily takes out a photograph of his fiancée, Liza, and again loses himself in the realm of fantasy: "Sighing, he put the picture and letters in his left side pocket and began to dream about his future married life. And these dreams seemed to him even more pleasant than the dreams about the statesman who would come to him to thank him for the good seed sown in his heart" (56).

With the noise of the sea, reality again asserts itself, destroying this dream also. Significantly, a steamship, which in the first paragraph of the story was "probably English," now becomes definite and real: "the English steamship moved out of the band of moonlight" (56).

At this point Vasily meets Kudryashov. In the ensuing confrontation between the two, which provides the main body of the story, we learn much about the latter from his words and from the detailed description of the material ambience which is a vital aspect of his characterization. However, we learn little of Vasily: there are no physical descriptions of him, nor does he speak a great deal in comparison to Kudryashov. What the latter says is recorded; what Vasily says is often not. Garshin will relate, for instance, how "Vasily spoke long and ardently" (66), without being any more specific. Thus to a great extent the reader's impression of Vasily is dependent on his primordial portrayal. The way he acts and interacts with Kudryashov will be compared and contrasted to the way he reacted to his own inner thoughts and subconscious motivations at the beginning of the story, and ultimately we are faced with the knotty problem of deciding whether Vasily's protests against Kudryashov's immorality are real and valid, or as illusionary as his dreams.

At first glance "The Meeting" resembles "The Tale of a Toad and a Rose" in its explicit oppositions. Vasily appears as positive and pure as the rose, Kudryashov as negative and repulsive as the toad. Such is not necessarily the case, however. The author's attitude toward Vasily Petrovich is at times ambiguous. He does not always side with Vasily; sometimes Garshin's point of view as narrator coincides with Kudryashov's.

As the story progresses Garshin develops the contrast between the former friends as they partake of a Gogolian repast of food and wine. Kudryashov is repeatedly struck by his friend's innocence, though annoyed by his criticism. Vasily Petrovich, in turn, is dismayed at his friend's lack of conscience. Each thinks back to the past, but here too their reactions differ completely. Vasily asks his friend to remember "about the student years, about the times, when life was good if not in a material sense, then in a moral sense" (59). But these years represent something else to Kudryashov, who replies: "Remember what? How we ate sausages made with dog meat?" (59).

This conversation further emphasizes the different planes on which these two former friends now move. Kudryashov is constantly concerned with his physical state; his deception of the government is important for him, because it enables him to satisfy his hedonistic impulses. His digressions during dinner deal frequently with his ability to obtain superior foods and wines. Vasily is more concerned with the spiritual side of his friend. He spends the meal either urging Kudryashov to come to his senses, or else lapsing into brief, silent periods only to return to his former sententious tone.

In the end, though, he is affected by one of Kudryashov's material possessions—his aquarium. This glittering symbol of Kudryashov's affluence and ostentatiousness succeeds where his pontificating failed; that is, it prevents even silent protestation on Vasily's part. Much as the sea in the opening led Vasily into dreams and illusions, so the aquarium distracts him from reality. To Kudryashov's assertion that immorality is nonsense, Vasily responds, "What's that?" (72); to his declaration about his former gnawings of conscience, Vasily replies, "Do as you will" (72). Vasily responds to both statements indifferently, as though no longer concerned with Kudryashov's iniquity, against which he had before reacted so sententiously.

In the concluding paragraph, when they return to the dining room, the servant, Ivan Pavlych is waiting with a bottle of champagne. As Karl Kramer asks,

Does this imply that Kudryashov may yet overcome Vasily's moral compunctions? We can never be sure [since] ultimately, the story treats not a moral issue but rather the relation between our belief and our identity: as one is altered, so is the other. The problem Garshin poses is the nature of our identity itself and the fragility of any assumption about what we are or will become.[3]

While this may be true to a certain extent, ultimately Garshin transcends the problem of identity alone and goes on to challenge the more general and more profound assumptions of our realities and our illusions. What is real and what is illusory about the conclusion of "The Meeting"? Vasily appraises the aquarium, representing as it does two distinct spheres of being, from two different standpoints. First, when he sees it lit only by the candle, it is calm, shadowy, vague, incomprehensible. But when the electric light is turned on, the fish tank is transformed by movement, complexity, coruscation. The transformation is so complete that Vasily "didn't recognize the aquarium" (70).

The new perception of the tank, however, exposes Kudryashov's creation for what it is—artifice. It is a simulated copy of a world which exists only within the narrow confines of his imagination. Kudryashov lives with the misconception that the aquarium is a microcosm of the real world, and he deludes himself into thinking that by imitating the creatures in the tank, he is thereby behaving more honestly than his fellow man. He tells Vasily, for example: "I love all these creatures because they are so honest, not like our brother—man. They devour one another and are not ashamed of it" (70). Kudryashov obviously feels that by candidly acknowledging his crimes and accepting responsibility for them, he is more sincere and honest than others, including Vasily.

While Garshin might have wanted his readers to draw analogies between the well-furnished fish tank and Kudryashov's equally well furnished apartment, any parallel between Kudryashov himself and his fish exists only in his mind. His argument in the conclusion is only a rationalization of those actions of his he has defended throughout the story. Garshin utilizes the same device for the opposite effect in "Signal" (The Signal). In this story one of the protagonists, Spiridov, proclaims that "there is not on the earth an animal more predatory and more evil than man. A wolf will not eat another wolf, but man will eat his fellow man" (302). Semyon objects to Spiridov's observation: "Well, brother, a wolf will eat another wolf, what are you saying?" (302). The underlying concept in both examples is that men are neither fish nor animals. Men concern themselves with morality and immorality; animals are amoral. The exception, of course, occurs, as it frequently does in Garshin, when he anthropomorphizes members of the animal and plant kingdoms, as in "The Frog Traveler," "Attalea princeps," and "That Which Never Was."

Fundamental moral commitments intrigue man, however, and Vasily demonstrates that man will question his own and other's

actions and ethics. It does not matter that "he is unable to prove
that Kudryashov is a criminal,"[4] as a contemporary critic wrote.
Whether or not the reader ascertains Vasily's final position is ir-
relevant. To Kramer's question directed toward the possibility of
Kudryashov's philosophy prevailing over Vasily's moral compunctions, we would reply that it is sufficient that Vasily had displayed
these moral compunctions in the first place.

As for Kudryashov's claim that the devouring of one fish by another is a natural as opposed to a moral act, Garshin makes his point
clear. The fish do not choose what they eat; they eat instinctively.
Man, on the other hand, does have a choice, a wide choice, as
Kudryashov's eating habits during the story illustrate. The fish live
in a world which is genuine to them, but illusory to a man who
would equate their physical and ethical worlds with his own. Vasily
lives under an illusion of morality, and while the reader never learns
whether Vasily converts to Kudryashov's way of thinking, he does
know that both men have been troubled enough to verbalize their
thoughts and articulate their convictions.

"The Meeting" allows Garshin to pose the questions of morality
versus immorality, reality versus illusion, and it is the posing of
these questions which is one of the author's primary objectives at
the close of the work. While Garshin's attitude toward Vasily and
Kudryashov is occasionally vague—this is especially the case with
Vasily's position in the conclusion—in the final analysis the author's
sympathy indeed lies with Vasily. This does not mean, of course,
that Vasily has not been affected by his meeting with Kudryashov.
He has. Consequently the story's ending contrasts sharply with its
opening. As Paul Varnai puts it, "No longer does the serene light
of the moon illumine Vasily Petrovich's perceptions, but the artificial
light fixtures of Kudryashov; the sea had promised freedom—the
waters of the aquarium show stagnation and confinement; the move-
ments of the colorful crowds observed by Vasily Petrovich on his
boulevard stroll has [sic] become transmogrified into the purpose-
less teeming of low animal life within the setting of garish, suffo-
cating fauna."[5]

II *"The Bears"* (1883)

"Medvedi" (The Bears) relates events which occur in the town
of Belsk during a short period in September 1857 as told sometimes

by a youth-narrator, sometimes by an omniscient narrator. Gypsies from four districts have been arriving in the town with their pet bears pursuant to a government order drawn up five years previously. Although the performing bears have been the gypsies' main source of support, the latter must now execute the former to satisfy the governmental decree. The gypsies appeal to the local constable for help, but, although in sympathy with them, he cannot countermand the order and the bears are executed by their owners amid a carnival atmosphere created by the local aristocracy, who watch the execution with a great deal of excitement. During the killing a young bear breaks loose and alarms the local inhabitants, but it is soon destroyed and the town returns to normal.

The ending of "The Bears" is anticlimactic. During the work the reader is given hints that something unexpected and dramatic will ensue: he learns that the town of Belsk is unusually excited, that the gypsies are to be armed with rifles, that the first bear, Potap, has been let loose for the execution. And, indeed, these expectations appear to be borne out when a young bear does break loose, sending the town into a frenzy.

But this represents the height of the action in the body of the story, for, as the author explains "the danger was really not very great" (214). The bear, it turns out, is more frightened than the villagers, and instead of inflicting injury, it becomes the object of overkill: "Everyone who had a rifle considered it his duty to plant a bullet in the dying beast, and when they skinned it it was not of any use" (215).

As the story unfolds the reader becomes aware that Garshin is not interested in the bears per se, so much as in the local aristocracy, in the gypsies, and in the effect the slaughter of the bears produces on both.

The story ends with an epilogue in which the narrator, following in the footsteps of Pushkin ("The Station Master") and Gogol ("The Tale of How Ivan Ivanovich Quarreled with Ivan Nikoforovich"), returns to the scene of the primary action to make his final comments, to tie the final threads, to express the concluding, ironic point of view.[6]

These concluding remarks deal with the gypsies only insofar as they close the circle of the gypsies' having become horsethieves. In the beginning of the story, Foma Fomich, the druggist, warns Olga Pavlovna, leader of the local "society," that if the bears are destroyed the gypsies will become horsethieves. Later when the gypsies plead their case to the constable, he informs them that he is unable to help them and acknowledges that now the townspeople will have to watch out for their horses. Finally, at the story's conclusion, we learn that within a week two horses were stolen from Foma Fomich.

Of course, the fact that the gypsies do become horsethieves is directly correlated to their having been forced by the authorities to kill their only means of legal livelihood—the bears. The irony of the situation is patent.

In contrast to the gypsies, whose plight intensified with the termination of events, conditions for the local aristocracy improve or, at worst, remain stable: the constable has received a promotion "for good management"; the brothers Isotov, as of old, shout in incorrect French *granron* and *orebur;* Foma Fomich, who benefited financially from the slaughter of the bears, has grown fatter. The main thrust of the ending, however, is concentrated on Olga Pavlovna. What effect has the destruction of the bears had on her? Olga has been able to buy large quantities of bear grease, a purported remedy for baldness. What has been the benefit of this? Garshin, so often concerned with our perception of illusion and reality, in the conclusion treats the subject in a comically ironic manner. Despite the fact that Olga Pavlovna has smeared her head with bear grease, her hair nevertheless has grown thinner, not thicker, and the narrator in a jocular tone adds, in the last sentence of the story, "Her chignon hides it so well, however, that positively nothing is noticeable" (216). Thus a potentially tragic tone is avoided in the ending by the author's pointed and humorous comments on the townspeople. The gypsies will survive—now as horsethieves; the townspeople will endure. Nothing has changed.

III   *"The Signal"* (1887)

"The Signal" concerns two railroad linemen, an old man, Semyon Ivanov, and a young one, Vasily Spiridov. Semyon, who has had a difficult life, enjoys his job, for all his needs are satisfied and, perhaps for the first time in his life, he is content. Spiridov is a hot-tempered individual who after being reprimanded for a minor breach of the railroad regulations complains to his superiors, at first locally, then in Moscow. Receiving no satisfaction, Spiridov tears

up a section of track, thereby hoping to avenge himself by derailing
a train. Semyon finds Vasily engaged in his vengeful act and makes
a red flag by dyeing a white scarf red with his own blood. Before
the train engineer sees the flag, Semyon, weak from loss of blood,
drops the flag, but Vasily appears to snatch up the flag and stop the
train. He then confesses.

In developing his story Garshin is careful to emphasize the contrasts between Semyon and Vasily. While we learn little of Vasily's
past, we do learn about Semyon's: his health is bad; he had served
as an orderly in the army during the Russo-Turkish War, where
three times a day he was forced to run in the open under enemy
fire to take tea to the officer he serves; when he returns from the
war, he finds that both his father and four-year-old son have died.
The officer with whom he served during the war eventually finds
him the job of lineman on the railroad, and Semyon is overjoyed
with his new means of livelihood. He has a new hut, as much
firewood as he needs, a small garden, and a job adequate for his
needs and suitable for his abilities. This is why Semyon has such
difficulty understanding Vasily's bitterness.

Semyon has trouble comprehending when Vasily argues, for example, that "there is no creature crueler than man. Were it not for
people's malice and greed—it would be possible to live" (302). But
as the events of the story unfold, Vasily's opinions seem borne out.
Once on an inspection tour, the rail inspector, drunk, fines Vasily
for planting cabbages without permission. Vasily vows to report the
inspector to the district chief during a subsequent inspection, which
he does, but instead of giving him satisfaction, the district chief
slaps him in the face. Vasily goes to Moscow to complain at the very
top, but returns a few days later without the satisfaction he so
desired.

Vasily seeks revenge then by ripping up a section of track, but
he is caught in the act by Semyon and runs away. Semyon immediately realizes the full extent of Vasily's wrath: a passenger train,
not a freight train, is shortly due; the derailment will occur on a
high embankment, so there will be a greater loss of life. To make
the impending disaster even more horrible, Semyon imagines the
third-class cars to be filled with children.

At first Semyon starts to run to his hut for tools; as a worker and
a dedicated employee, he thinks first in terms of fixing the track.
He immediately realizes, however, that he has too little time, so

he returns to the tracks, buries a knife in his arm, soaks a white scarf in his own blood, ties the "red flag" to a stick and attempts to stop the train. Semyon faints from loss of blood, but a hand reaches out, grabs the flag, and stops the train. The hand belongs to Vasily, who, obviously affected by Semyon's heroic example, has returned to avert a disaster. When the train stops Vasily exclaims: "Tie me up. I have pulled up a rail" (307).

IV A Feeling of Helplessness

The three works discussed above are similar in that in each Garshin presents a hero who is reduced to helplessness and frustration by external events over which he has no control.

Thus Vasily Petrovich, initially a vocal critic of Kudryashov's actions, is ultimately silenced both by his own inability to prove to Kudryashov the immorality of his deeds and by the continuous display of Kudryashov's affluence, ending, finally, with the aquarium. Helpless and frustrated by his inability to silence Kudryashov, Vasily is himself silenced.

In the next two stories, the levels of frustration are so intensified as to result in extraordinary behavior. It is clear to all concerned that the decision to execute the bears is inane and unfair, and the ineluctable consequences of that decision substantiate this. The gypsies, normally peaceful, honest nomads, become thieves when familiar means of livelihood are taken from them.

Vasily Spiridov is also forced by external, unfair circumstances to respond in an abnormal manner. Garshin points out the inequitable application of the regulations by the superiors: Semyon works a vegetable garden left by the former lineman, while Spiridov is reprimanded by his superiors for raising vegetables. When the rail inspector tells Spiridov to rip out his cabbages, the superior is drunk, for he ignores them when sober. When fiery, unpredictable Spiridov is wronged, he responds in a rather drastic manner by complaining to the superior's superiors and is further suppressed, at which point he rebels. When his frustration reaches the breaking point, he tears up the section of track.

The three miscellaneous stories are further distinguished by a much greater concern on the author's part with plot and expectation. In each work the story line seems to develop more traditionally, with events building toward an anticipated climax. Thus we expect the bears and/or gypsies to rebel, to strike out against an unjust, foolish decree. Instead the story ends with a discussion of bear grease and its relative merits in impeding the spread of baldness. We expect some dramatic result to flow from the chance meeting between Vasily Petrovich and Kudryashov. As the two friends eat their luxurious dinner, we look for some kind of resolution—Vasily might leave the house as a sign of protest; Kudryashov might bring Vasily into the affluent world of corruption. Instead, we get silence in the closing scene.

In "The Signal," too, there is a prominent story line: event is connected to event, building toward a high point which is actually realized when Vasily tears up the section of track. Vasily's Christian act in the finale, however, is a surprise.

In his day Garshin was viewed for the most part as a social writer, and Soviet critics continue to interpret him this way. "The Signal" is especially good proof of this contention. Garshin, however, was as much concerned with the mode of presentation of his stories as with their content, and while some are social in inclination others are concerned with universal themes transcending specific temporal and cultural limitations.

We have chosen to discuss Garshin's stories thematically, grouping together works with common themes. We might also have categorized his stories on the basis of their narrative techniques: the military tales, with the exception of "The Orderly and the Officer," are first-person narratives; the fairy tales are related by a third-person narrator, as are the miscellaneous stories; the artist/prostitute works are structured on dual first-person narratives, usually in diary form.[7]

Garshin's use of varied narrative techniques demonstrates, we believe, his careful interest in matching theme with technique, content with craft. This concern, along with his innate artistic talent, elevates Garshin above the level of social writer as that term was used in the 1870s and 1880s, when social literature was considered virtually synonymous with tendentious literature.

As a writer Garshin was not so much concerned with "message," with events, with the presentation and the solution of social and other problems. Instead, he was more interested in developing within his stories an inner rather than an outer tension.

CHAPTER 7

The Structure of the Garshinian Short Story

I *The Hero as Focus*

G ARSHIN shows a marked propensity for using the same characters in different stories. Thus a character with the surname
Ivanov, and with remarkably similar traits, appears in five different
stories: "Four Days," "From the Reminiscences of Private Ivanov,"
"The Signal," "The Orderly and the Officer," and "Otryvok iz neiz-
dannoi povesti" (An Excerpt from an Unpublished Story, published
in 1922; date of composition unknown). Ensign Stebelkov and his
orderly Nikita appear in "The Orderly and the Officer" and in "From
the Reminiscences of Private Ivanov." The prostitute Nadezhda
Nikolaevna appears in the story of the same name and in "An Occurrence." Critics have occasionally faulted Garshin for this on the
grounds that it indicated a lack of originality and inventiveness.[1]

Garshin, however, was apparently not concerned with inventing
new names or new characters for each story, because he was intentionally creating character types. Ensign Stebelkov, for example,
comes to represent a young officer new to military service;[2] a character named Masha is representative of a young girl, the object of
another character's love.

Not only do these particular types possess common characteristics, but almost all of Garshin's heroes are endowed by their creator
with the same basic traits. "All of Garshin's stories are closely tied
to one another . . . everywhere under various names, there appear,
in essence, one and the same hero,"[3] a critic wrote a few years after
Garshin's death. Since the structure of each story revolves around
the hero, it is necessary to examine and analyze him as a type who
will be a major focus of each work.

The typical hero is introspective. A Garshinian story is more often concerned with the thought processes of the hero (his inner world) than with the external forces acting on him (his outer world). Garshin emphasizes this through his narrative techniques—inner monologue, first-person narratives, often in the form of reminiscences, diaries, etc.—although even in third-person narratives the omniscient narrator concentrates on internal thoughts. An example:

Vasily Petrovich ate and thought, thought and ate. He was greatly confused and really did not know what to do. As a matter of principle, he ought to leave his old friend's house and never set foot in it again. "This piece of meat is stolen," he thought, having placed it in his mouth and having sipped the wine poured for him by his obliging host. "And that which I myself am doing? thought the poor teacher, but his thoughts remained only thoughts and behind them hid a certain secret voice, which objected to each thought with: "Well, what then?" And Vasily Petrovich felt that he was not in a position to decide this question and continued to sit. "Well, I will observe"—flashed through his mind in self-justification, after which he was ashamed of himself. "Why should I observe; am I a writer?" (61–62)

This quotation illustrates several major characteristics of the Garshinian hero: his indecision and vacillation, his self-justification, his confusion over his moral principles, and his introspection. The hero is forced to be introspective, because he is usually faced with a moral dilemma: the hero of "Four Days" asks himself why he killed the Turk; the heroine of "An Occurrence" wonders whether to marry her so-called benefactor; the hero of "The Coward" debates with himself whether he is a coward; the hero of "A Night" must decide whether he will escape from his muddle by suicide.

This moral dilemma is sometimes resolved as when the narrator in "The Coward" finds he is not a coward; sometimes it is not—the narrator of "Four Days" never decides quite why he killed. But it makes little difference whether the moral dilemma is resolved, for Garshin is primarily intrigued by the actual process of handling it. He is concerned with the manner in which external actions and interactions with other characters are reflected in the minds of his heroes, who are then forced to rethink and reevaluate their choices. This creates the basic flow of the Garshinian story.

In "Four Days," for example, the events leading up to the murder and the murder itself are dispensed with in one page. The story's significance lies in Ivanov's reaction to the murder, in his ponderings on war and death, in his expectation of an almost surely imminent death. There is little action or plot; rather the story is a series of thoughts, impressions, musings—all centered in Ivanov's mind, all filtered through his perceptions.

This internal concentration is reinforced by the usual isolation of the hero who, even when surrounded by fellow beings, feels cut off and separated from others. Garshin's heroes are usually rootless city dwellers, alienated from society and from one another.

The underlying causes of this isolation may vary somewhat from hero to hero: with Vasily Petrovich ("The Meeting") it is moral in nature; with Nikita ("The Orderly and the Officer") it is social; with Ryabinin ("The Artists") it is philosophical. However, the primary type of isolation common to each hero is psychological. Each hero is forced to confront his moral dilemma alone, and it is the psychological effects of the hero's inner struggle which interest Garshin.

The reason for his hero's isolation is of no importance to Garshin. He does not tell us how or why, for example, Nadezhda Nikolaevna became a prostitute, or the causes of the madman's insanity in "The Red Flower." Soviet criticism to the contrary notwithstanding, Garshin is a psychological, not a sociological, writer. The causes of prostitution or prostitution as a social ill is not Garshin's focus; instead, he concentrates on the thoughts and actions of a woman who just happens to be a prostitute. Similarly, Garshin does not make the madman a symbol for a revolutionary,[4] but instead develops the relationship between the madman and the real, sane world which surrounds him. The emphasis in this story is so clearly on the actions and reactions of the madman as he wanders through the worlds of reality and fantasy that to assign him the allegorical role of revolutionary detracts from Garshin's artistry: then the stress would be on the outcome, on some higher message, instead of on the madman's treatment.

While Garshin does not always provide physical descriptions and extensive biographies of his heroes, he does delve into the mental states of his protagonists. His heroes are often in anxious states, suffering mental torment and pain. Faced with external events, the heroes internalize them and, lacking psychological releases for their failures, frustrations, and inadequacies, they turn ever inward toward further anguish. They attempt to escape their torment by articulating a desire not to think, since thinking is a partial cause of their anxiety and pain: Ryabinin seeks a new subject for a painting because tormenting questions and thoughts "disappear during pe-

riods of work" (67); Nadezhda Nikolaevna strives to escape from
oppressive thoughts by trying not to think. But the hero's misfortune
lies in the fact that he cannot escape his consciousness or, even
worse, his conscience.

The hero strives for release, but his psychological makeup is such
that his efforts are usually blocked and release never comes. The
Soviet scholar Grigory Byaly feels that "the sufferings and torments
of Garshin's heroes are engendered more by the characteristics of
their personal psychology than by the conditions of their public
lives."[5] This is certainly a valid and, coming as it does from a Soviet
critic, brave observation. Though it is axiomatic that the hero's
personal psychology is of great value, the character of the Garshinian
hero is more complex, for he always acts in conjunction with some
representative of society who is in a position different from his own,
a counter focus. Thus the hero is isolated, but he is not confined
to a vacuum. To take an example from "The Meeting," it is Kudryashov's differing viewpoint of what is permissible in society as
opposed to Vasily Petrovich's which engenders Vasily's dilemma.
He tries to express the torment he feels over Kudryashov's actions,
but Kudryashov does not accept his arguments and instead projects
them back to Vasily, who then is disturbed both by Kudryashov's
actions and his own.

The typical hero, passive by nature, accepts his suffering as a
concomitant part of his situation because he can always imagine
other conditions even more horrible than his own. Thus Ivanov
does not shout out when he hears voices because if they are Turks
his lot will be worse; Nadezhda ("An Occurrence") does not marry
Ivan Ivanovich, for a future life with him may be worse than her
present one.

When the hero does move from passivity to activity, the result
is usually disastrous: the palm tree accomplishes her goal and breaks
through the greenhouse roof to the blue sky beyond only to die;
the narrator in "The Coward" goes to war only to be killed by a
stray bullet; Andrey kills Bessonov, but loses his beloved, Nadezhda
Nikolaevna, in the process.

The hero in Garshin is passive and isolated because he does not
fit into the society around him. He is often a social outcast. The
heroes of "Four Days" and "The Coward" are scorned by their
friends for volunteering for military service. The officers ("From
the Reminiscenses of Private Ivanov") cannot understand Ivanov's

desire to live in the same tent with common soldiers. Thus the hero, often acting in a way that evokes bewilderment on the part of his fellows, is in turn puzzled by the fact that others do not understand him. This lack of understanding accentuates the hero's inability to fit into the society around him.

The hero's alienation, however, is not always of his own choosing. Often he is afraid of the life around him. The rose fears not death per se, but death at the hands of the toad. Aleksey Petrovich ("A Night") is unable "to live any longer engrossed in his fears" (116). Aleksey Petrovich is idealistic, but his idealism does not help him to live in a world which he fears. He is disgusted with himself and with his fears, but instead of striking out, he withdraws further into himself and separates himself from the world around him. The point is, however, that his withdrawal is involuntary; he is no longer able to cope with society.

Whether the hero's alienation is voluntary or involuntary, his estrangement is often manifested in his distorted and strange view of society and the world at large. Frequently the hero observes reality through a haze or is in a dreamlike state. Ivanov ("From the Reminiscences of Private Ivanov") remembers a march as through a dream. Ryabinin is enveloped by a mist; a mist also obscures the narrator in "A Very Short Romance." Lopatin sees through a bluish haze. It is not only the visual sense which is affected in this way, but also the aural. The hero has a keen sense of hearing, and Garshin saturates his stories with references to sounds of the external world. Moreover, in addition to external sounds, the hero perceives inner sounds. Ivanov ("Four Days"), Nadezhda Nikolaevna ("An Occurrence"), and Semyon ("The Signal") all hear a ringing in their ears. Lopatin, Ryabinin, and Aleksey Petrovich hear internal sounds.

Thanks, perhaps, to his feeling of estrangement from society, the hero often looks back to his childhood, which in Garshin's works assumes an idyllic character. Orphaned from a society he cannot' understand, he recalls the days when life was simpler, thoughts were fewer. It is interesting that most of Garshin's heroes are orphans in the biological sense of the word, too. If a hero mentions parents, he mentions a father or a mother, for often one or both of the parents died when the hero was young. Only one protagonist, Nadezhda Nikolaevna, seems to have both parents alive. The author has done this in order to add a note of social irony: Nadezhda comes from a respectable family and is well educated, but still she has become a prostitute.

The heroes summon up fond memories of childhood. Ryabinin remembers being comforted by his mother when he was a frightened child. In the present, as a grown man, he is alone with no one to comfort him. Nadezhda Nikolaevna recollects playing in the steppe when spring was resurrecting life with splashes of color. This memory comes to her as she stands one spring day on the bank of the Neva, but the present St. Petersburg spring pales by comparison with the recollected spring.

The discrepancy between the imagined past and the real present is further evidence of the hero's disillusionment with his life and with his society. This discrepancy also points to the melancholy and feelings of hopelessness which are part of the hero's view of self. The hero's inner feelings many times are externally manifested through tears and cries, but for the most part he views himself more in moral, spiritual, and psychological terms than in physical ones. The way the hero views himself is a continuous process; his vacillations open up to the reader the many facets of the hero's character. The reader becomes aware and reacts as the hero himself becomes aware and reacts. As a result our impressions are based on a constantly changing pattern of action and reaction, concentrated in a specific hero, based on a specific act, but broadened by the hero's use of analogy to project himself into a larger reality. Thus the coward, in observing Kuzma Fomich, generalizes Kuzma's suffering, expanding it into the general suffering of all men dying in war. Nadezhda Nikolaevna generalizes her hatred of a few to a hatred of all. The madman transforms a guard's simple action into an organized conspiracy against him.

The generalizing of events from the hero's viewpoint further emphasizes his role as the focus of each work. He is the epicenter of each story. Events and thoughts are presented through the subjective prism of his consciousness. Also present in each work, however, is a counterfocus, a foil to the hero, and it is the interaction between these two foci which creates the action and the tension in each work.

II *The Foil as Counterfocus*

Garshin's stories are not necessarily predicated on a symmetrical structure. Though the hero and foil each represent a different focus, the foci are not always of equal value. The hero is usually the predominant character in the work, but not always. Dedov receives more attention than Ryabinin ("The Artists"), although the latter is the hero. The foil may be of equal value to the hero—Stebelkov and Nikita ("The Orderly and the Officer")—or he may be of lesser value, as in the case of the director in "Attalea princeps."

Whatever the spacial proportions may be, structurally the foil's role is of utmost significance. This is clearly seen in "Four Days."The foil to the hero, Ivanov, in this story is the Turk, who becomes the main focal point for the hero. After his first contact with the Turk, Ivanov begins to distinguish between two separate worlds: "A whole picture brightly flashes in my mind. This was a long time ago: though all, all of my life, *that* life, when I did not lie here with broken legs, was so long ago" (6).[6] The foil becomes the center of this new, small world which encapsulates Ivanov. The latter is drawn to his victim by thirst and repelled by his putrefying smell, which throughout the story emphasizes the Turk's presence. He is a constant focal point attracting Ivanov's gaze; this in turn motivates Ivanov to think about his victim and his act, in addition to providing a point-counterpoint for Ivanov's inner monologue.[7]

The physical and mental anguish Ivanov endures is manifested by thirst and conscience, which possess his mind by turns. In this, as in most of Garshin's stories, the foil is connected to the hero on two planes: the physical and the psychological. In the present instance the foil provides relief for Ivanov's physical suffering on the one hand, but intensifies his mental anguish on the other.

Much as the albatross in Samuel Coleridge's *The Rime of the Ancient Mariner,* the Turk as victim is also the symbol of atonement. As the mariner wears the albatross around his neck, so Ivanov is forced to witness the day-by-day decomposition of his victim. When the mariner has partially repented, he obtains water in the form of rain from heaven; when Ivanov has, he gets the water in the Turk's flask. Ivanov's atonement is not an oral acknowledgment of wrongdoing, but rather an empathizing with his victim and even a desire to accept the Turk's fate himself: "I would even change places with him" (7).

Ivanov, like the mariner, is rescued only after many tribulations. With Ivanov, however, these are all connected to the ever-present disintegrating foil. As a matter of fact, salvation does not come for Ivanov until the Turk has lost his original form and become a mass of maggots and bones, or to use Ivanov's phrase, a "skeleton in uniform."

An analogous situation is described in Coleridge's poem. Death and Life-in-Death throw dice for the mariner and the crew with the result that Death wins the crew and Life-in-Death wins the mariner. As a consequence the mariner is forced to witness the death, one by one, of the two hundred crew members.

In "Four Days" there is a parallel development between the hero and the foil. As the latter's position worsens, so does the former's. Critics often refer to the scenes of the decaying corpse to demonstrate Garshin's antiwar attitude in portraying war in all its horrible reality, but these descriptions have a more sophisticated function. They are carefully worked into the structure of the story and are important for the effect they have on the hero and for the depiction of the parallelism and contrast between the two.

Ivanov describes the foil three times on the third day of his ordeal. The first description, early in the morning, contains specific physical evidence of the decomposition of the Turk as man:

Yes, he was horrible. His hair had begun to fall out. His skin, black by nature, has begun to pale and turn yellow: his swollen face has stretched to such an extent that it is splitting behind the ears. Maggots were swarming there. His feet, tightly laced up in his boots, have swollen, and huge blisters have been pushed out between the grommets of the boots. He has swollen like a mountain. What will the sun do to him today? (10)

Garshin underscores the connection between the foil and the hero by specifically mentioning the Turk's swollen legs, a reminder that Ivanov has been wounded in both legs. He realizes and repeatedly asserts that the Turk's fate will be his own. He is therefore prodded into action, crawling away to try to escape the overpowering smell of the corpse which is prophetic of his own imminent death. But he cannot escape it totally. He vomits. He cries. All are actions in response to seeing the foil. This foil as death (the connection with death is always a *sine qua non* of the foil in Garshin's works) evokes in the hero a desire to live.

This desire to live prevents Ivanov from calling out to the intruders. The risk of torture more horrible than that which he is enduring, and certain death—though his own death seems certain in any case—deters him from risking a call. When he realizes the intruders are friends, not foes, it is too late. When he spills the water accidentally and apparently loses his last tie to life, his fate seems sealed. It is then that he casts his second glance at his neighbor:

Once, when I opened my eyes, in order to look at him, I became horrified. He no longer had a face. It had slid from the bones. A terrible bony smile, the eternal smile, seemed to me so loathsome, so horrible, that I have never seen anything like it, although as a medical student I have many times held skulls in my hands in preparation for experiments. (12)

The humanoid features of the corpse have been lost; the metaphoric, synecdochic description stresses its non-human aspects.

Between the second and third descriptions of the corpse comes the latter half of the "dog tale." In the first part of this tale, the reader is told of a small dog run over by a streetcar. The dog is still alive when a man carries her away, leaving the impression that she is saved. The reader now learns that the dog was not saved at all; rather the man smashed her against a wall and threw her into an empty bin, where she suffered for a whole day before dying. The parallel between her fate and Ivanov's is patent. The final description of the Turk most vividly depicts his final end and Ivanov's: "He is completely distended. Myriads of worms fall from him. How they swarm! When he is disposed of and nothing remains but bone and uniform, then it will be my turn. And I shall wind up in the same way" (13).

But Ivanov does not experience the same fate as the Turk. He is rescued, and though he suffers the loss of a leg he survives, like the ancient mariner, to tell his story of suffering and anguish to others. For the mariner this is his penance, and he finds temporary relief from his guilt in telling his story. Perhaps Garshin intends the same thing for Ivanov, who cannot escape his feelings of guilt: "Murder, murderer. . . . And who? I!" (9).

In "The Coward" the foil is Kuzma Fomich and the hero is the narrator. While Garshin based this story on fact, he made one major change in writing the story. In a letter to his mother of March 12, 1876, he describes the fate which has befallen one of his friends.

We are griefstricken: one of my friends, Kvitka, is dying. He had a simple boil on his cheek, one so huge that his face was distorted on one side. On Saturday Karrik, his doctor, came to lance the boil: after examining him, he became troubled and went for a surgeon. He brought Eberman, who lanced it. Karrik had become troubled because poor Semyon had a black spot below the boil (between the neck and left breast): it was gangrene.[8]

Garshin describes the events of the next two days—the progress of the disease and his part in caring for Kvitka—and then continues:

On the third day, Tuesday, there was still hope: the gangrene had stopped. But yesterday when Dolinin and Marya Dmitrievna and I began to wash the wound, we noticed with horror two more black spots. The doctors come every day—Karrik two times, Eberman one. They have already told Semyon that he has only three or four days to live. By the time you receive this letter, he will be dead.[9]

The fate of the real Kvitka runs basically parallel to that of the fictional Kuzma. But in a letter to his mother a week later, Garshin joyously proclaimed: "A miracle has occurred: Kvitka has recovered!"[10] Thus, as in "Four Days," Garshin has manipulated the real and the imaginary. The real person lives while the fictional character dies from the same case of gangrene. Garshin needs his death for the story. Kuzma is one of the structural foci of the work, and his death is required for the effect it has on, and for the parallelism it shows to, the hero, the coward-narrator.

It should be stressed here that although affinities do exist, and although there are often times when the hero's and foil's fates seem similar or identical, the two are separate and distinct entities. The foil is not an alter ego or a double of the hero. The symbiotic hero-foil relationship in "Four Days" and the similarity of fates of hero-foil in "The Coward" are merely variants of an authorial device. Most of Garshin's stories are based on hero-foil relationships, relationships formed from the interaction of two structurally separate epicenters, but these interdependent associations are not always handled in precisely the same manner.

Obviously, if the presentations were identical in each story, Garshin's works would be monotonously similar, with little artistic value or interest. Such is not the case. While the stories do fall into classifiable categories, the fact that certain stories may be discussed under the rubric "military tale," for example, does not mean that they all treat the soldier or war in the same way. The originality in each Garshinian story lies in the way the author introduces and develops the hero-foil lines, in the way he presents these lines against the tale's general background.

"The Red Flower" is a case in point. Here the hero is a madman, the foil a flower; the relationship between them is a life-and-death struggle resulting in the death of both. In "Attalea princeps" the foil, the director, is victorious over the palm tree hero. In "The Tale of a Toad and a Rose" the toad-foil is unsuccessful while the rose-hero triumphs.

The main structural role of the foil is to occupy a point independent of the hero, yet to interact with him in creating the action, flow, and tension of the story. The foil may accomplish this in various ways. He need not literally do something to evoke a reaction. The Turk's primary action is to decompose, but this is sufficient to create a pivot for Ivanov's imagination. In "The Tale of a Toad and A Rose" all physical action is accomplished by the toad. In response to his attacks, the rose can only respond with emotions—horror, disgust, fright—and with exclamations—"Oh Lord, if only I could die a different death!" (221).

The hero is often attracted by the foil and simultaneously repelled by him. Ivanov speaks of the Turk, dead and bloodstained, yet wishes he could change places with him. Nadezhda Nikolaevna refuses Ivan Ivanovich's offer of marriage and is repelled by the drunkenness which she directly causes, while at the same time she responds to his letter and appears in his room dressed in a manner she knows will appeal to him. Vasily Petrovich rejects Kudryashov's admitted immoral behavior, but is overawed—"What taste, effect!" (71)—by his aquarium, obtained precisely through his immoral acts.

The Garshinian hero as a type is often presented in an idealized form. He is a sensitive, unprepossessing, manipulated individual who is basically moral and righteous. To vary this stereotype somewhat, Garshin depicts his hero as attracted to a frequently evil aspect of the foil. Lopatin, for example, is cast in the mold of the heroic type, while Bessonov exemplifies the typical foil; nevertheless, there is an undeniable attraction between the two, and they possess many similar characteristics. Lopatin and Bessonov love the same girl, erupt in the same physical and emotional outbursts, and eventually commit murder as a consequence of the same love obsession. Each misjudges the other's capabilities. Each looks on the other as possessing character traits unlike his own when in reality their personalities are often congruent.

The hero-foil relationship is thus a functional device by which the author develops a character in a less direct manner. Garshin introduces the hero's darker side tangentially, thus making his portrayal more complex without actually destroying his truly positive nature.

Usually the foil colors the hero by dissimilarity. The hero, for example, may exemplify introspection, the foil loquaciousness. In "An Occurrence" Nadezhda Nikolaevna communicates with the reader through her inner thoughts while Ivan Ivanovich's opinions are expressed in his conversations with Evsey Evseich and with Nadezhda. In "The Meeting" Vasily Petrovich ponders, Kudryashov verbalizes. The foil's cynicism may contrast with the hero's idealism. Lopatin's gentle outlook on the world clashes with Bessonov's; Semyon's love and respect for his fellow man are rejected by Vasily in "The Signal." The hero's failure may be presented against the background of the foil's success. The hero in Garshin's works is basically a failure; the foil is mostly successful in his endeavors. Thus Vasily's poverty prevents his marriage, while Kudryashov is financially solvent; Dedov is successful in the world of art and wins a gold medal while Ryabinin fails; Ivan Ivanovich succeeds in taking his own life, while Nadezhda fails to stop him. The hero's lack of success has even been equated by one scholar[11] to the trials of Sisyphus.

Although the foil frequently provides a contrasting backdrop for the hero, his is not always a diametrically opposed focus. On occasion the foil may even have certain traits in common with the hero. Kuzma Fomich possesses the same virtuous qualities as the narrator of "The Coward." We feel as sorry for Stebelkov and his life as we do for Nikita and his. The foils may be cynical, but they may sometimes be as idealistic as the heroes: cf. Ivan Ivanovich and Kuzma Fomich.

Just as the hero weeps frequently in stressful situations, so do some of the foils. Ivan cries over his relationship with Nadezhda; Ventsel sheds tears for his wounded and dead soldiers. Their common suffering forms a strong bond between hero and foil: in Garshin's stories all characters suffer, the heroes as well as the foils— even those who seem the most cynical and the most contented, such as Bessonov and Ventsel.

The foil is essential to the hero for a variety of reasons. For one thing, self-sacrifice is a basic motif in Garshin's works. As evidenced by the narrator of "The Coward," Semyon Ivanov ("The Signal"), and Nikita Ivanov ("The Orderly and the Officer"), it is the hero who usually sacrifices himself for the sake of the foil. The madman loses his life, the narrator of "The Coward" washes Kuzma's wound, Semyon suffers injury in helping Vasily, Nikita serves at the whim and command of Stebelkov.

Perhaps the major function of the foil, though, is to contrast with the hero as a type. Unlike the hero, the foil is not a type; or rather, *because* the hero is a type, the foil cannot be. The interaction of the same two types in each story would be too monotonous, a pitfall which Garshin avoids by making each foil different. Since the foils often serve as contrasts to the heroes, they must occasionally possess common attributes, but these are not sufficiently numerous or important to typify the foil. While the heroes possess virtually identical natures and exhibit the same emotions and responses, the foils do differ. Indeed, it is the individualized foil who provides much of the originality for each story, especially in Garshin's later works.

The heroes often need the counterbalance which the foils provide. Though some heroes are capable of standing by themselves as characters—e.g., Ivanov ("Four Days") or the madman ("The Red Flower")—most of them need the foil. Vasily Petrovich needs a Kudryashov, someone to challenge his previously unchallenged moral viewpoint, to force him to reevaluate his ideas of good and evil, to defend what he thinks is right. Kudryashov shows up Vasily's moral statements for what they are—trite platitudes. Without him Vasily is an impotent dreamer lost in a world of illusions. Kudryashov, certainly the more interesting and vibrant of the two, compels Vasily to face life in all its horrifying complexity.

Likewise the foil Ventsel is more interesting and more believable than the hero Ivanov. The latter is a stylized, idealized young man of noble birth who enlists in the army and serves with the peasant soldiers in an attempt to get to know and understand them. He is presented as so positive as to be flat. Ventsel, on the other hand, though depicted as somewhat of a villain, is a fuller and more interesting character. As a matter of fact, Ventsel fits Edward M. Forster's requirement of roundness exactly: "The test of a round character is whether it is capable of surprising in a convincing way. If it never surprises, it is flat."[12]

Despite the negative traits inherent in Ventsel's personality, we also learn of his positive attributes: his love of poetry, his earlier feelings of respect and love for the peasant-soldier, and, in the final scene, his terrible remorse over the soldiers he has lost. Without Ventsel this story would lose its interest and become merely the portrait of an ideal figure.

Such was not Garshin's intent. The work is a series of impressions recounted by this idealized narrator, but the narrator's character is shaded and enhanced by the foil. And while Garshin is certainly fascinated with the narrator's impressions of war, he is also greatly concerned with the interplay of the two main characters.

Of course, if each story were based solely on a hero-foil relationship, Garshin's originality would soon suffer, so he frequently adds other structural levels. In the "Tale of a Toad and a Rose," the toad-rose relationship is tied to the sister-brother kinship. In "The Coward" the narrator and Kuzma interact with Lvov and Marya Petrovna. In the structurally most complex story "Nadezhda Nikolaevna," Garshin builds a complicated series of parallels around the primary association of Lopatin and Bessonov. The main tension derives from the conflict between these two, but subcurrents are developed in the love affairs between Lopatin and Sonya, Lopatin and Nadezhda, Bessonov and Nadezhda and the semihomosexual relationship between Lopatin and Gelfreykh.

III *Apropos of a Literary Controversy*

Garshin's use of the hero-foil interactions is helpful in understanding a literary controversy which has arisen over interpreting Garshin's works from either an inner or an outer point of view. Alexander Skabichevsky, on the one hand, thought Garshin a writer who dealt with the inner world: "Garshin really had very little concern with the external world. He disregarded external descriptions of characters and objects and paid attention primarily to the inner world of the heroes, to what they thought, felt and experienced in their souls."[13] Where Garshin's stories are concerned, Skabichevsky's ideas certainly seem valid. Who can dispute the concentration on the inner world of the Garshinian hero? Garshin's stories are, for the most part, psychological, based on thought processes, on emotions, on feelings.

Korney Chukovsky, however, with some justification, has challenged Skabichevsky's assumptions:

His strength does not at all lie in "shouting," but in a clear, serene picture, in the portrayal of the "outer," "external" world. Garshin is always "above," on the surface, among "the subjects of a subjective world," and to him is accessible only that which he is able to see, to classify, to feel. I am amazed that no one has yet noticed this, that he is a poet of sight, of visual images, and that his realm begins here. Not to exclaim but to describe—that is the basic requirement of his talent.[14]

Chukovsky's interpretations are also valid. Is it possible to deny the importance of description in Garshin's works? The descriptions of the Turk, of Kuzma's gangrene, of the toad, or of war are indispensable ingredients in their respective stories.[15]

How then do we reconcile these two opposing viewpoints? The answer is that neither critic is correct. Garshin is a writer of the inner world; Garshin is a writer of the outer world. The foil is the bridge between the two.

The foil is almost always a manifestation of the external, readily apparent world. Garshin provides very few physical descriptions of the hero but many of the foil. Aside from the glaring example of Ivanov and the Turk, there are instances such as "The Meeting," in which many descriptions of the physical reality surrounding Kudryashov are presented. Indeed, Kudryashov's character is delineated almost as much by the material goods around him, from his clothes at the beginning to his aquarium at the end, as by his dialogue with Vasily Petrovich. Vasily, on the other hand, is depicted entirely through his thoughts, his responses. There are no physical descriptions to aid the reader in evaluating Vasily and his actions.

The foil in Garshin is always externalized, always a projection of the physical, the material. This accounts for the vivid descriptions of Kuzma's chest wound or the Turk's face actually sliding off the bones. The physical action of the story is based on the collision between the hero and foil: Ivanov thrusts his bayonet into the Turk; the coward cleanses Kuzma's wound; the madman plucks the flower.

From this physical plane, the foil becomes a bridge to the higher, psychological plane. The hero must step back from the external to evaluate and reevaluate his actions. His collision with life on the physical plane forces him to examine psychological effects and results carefully. Though physical suffering is frequently an effect, the heroes suffer more mentally. Ivanov exclaims that his grief is worse than his wounds; the madman cries out more from his psychological torment than from the physical abuse he receives.

The psychological experiences of the hero evoked and extended by the foil provide Garshin's stories (especially the military tales and tales of madness) with movement and inner force. In thus moving from a traditional concern with plot to a greater concern with mood and tension, Garshin was breaking new ground in the development of the Russian short story.

CHAPTER 8

In the Shadow of Giants: Literary Influences

I Introduction

W HEN Vsevolod Garshin began publishing his short stories, he did so in the shadow of giants, but the giants casting these shadows would soon be gone. Ivan Turgenev, Leo Tolstoy, Fedor Dostoevsky, the three greatest Russian novelists—indeed, three of the greatest writers in the pantheon of world literature—would soon end their literary endeavors (Tolstoy temporarily, Turgenev and Dostoevsky permanently) and the Russian reading public would witness the end of an era and the decline of a genre.

Born within a decade of each other (Turgenev, 1818, Dostoevsky, 1821; Tolstoy, 1828), they began their prose careers within a few years of each other: Turgenev published "Khor and Kalinych" in 1847, Dostoevsky's "Poor People" appeared in 1846, and Tolstoy published "Childhood" in 1852. They also ended their careers within a few years of each other: Dostoevsky died in 1881 and Turgenev in 1883, while Leo Tolstoy underwent a religious crisis during this period when he finished A Confession and abandoned creative literature for several years.

With their deaths ended an outpouring of great novels of a quality and variety never before produced by any culture. In the twenty-five-year period from 1856 to 1881, an educated Russian had access to the following masterpieces of Russian literature (for the most part serialized in the "thick journals": Turgenev's Rudin (1856), A Nest of Gentlefolk (1859), On the Eve (1860), Fathers and Sons (1862), Smoke (1867), Virgin Soil (1877); Dostoevsky's Notes From the Underground (1864), Crime and Punishment (1866), The Idiot (1868), The Devils (also translated as The Possessed [1871]), A Raw Youth

(1875), *The Brothers Karamazov* (1880); Tolstoy's *The Cossacks* (1863), *War and Peace* (1865), *Anna Karenina* (1875); Goncharov's *Oblomov* (1859); Leskov's *Cathedral Folk* (1872); Saltykov-Shchedrin's *The Golovlyov Family* (1876).

The writing of these works coincided with the reign of Alexander II (1855–1881) and to a large extent the historical and political climate of the times encouraged the writing of novels. Alexander II, in contrast to his predecessor Nicholas I (1825–1855), relaxed the requirements of censorship, and under his leadership Russia looked to the future in expectation of change. Alexander's most important act was the emancipation of the serfs in 1861, though throughout his reign he introduced changes in other areas: the military, the courts, and in the realm of self-governance through the *zemstva* (local assemblies and boards).

To be sure, censorship existed, as did exile and/or prison for those who too boldly overstepped the limits established by the government, but still the writers of this period enjoyed a freedom not experienced by their literary forefathers, and critical essays of the most radical critics—Nikolay Chernyshevsky, Nikolay Dobrolubov, and Dmitry Pisarev—which would never have seen the light during Nicholas's rule appeared in print during the reign of Alexander II.

Other factors made the novel the dominant genre of this time. Prominent among them was the literary method of Realism. Writers attempted to depict life as it was, and therefore created huge fictional structures with numerous characters (*War and Peace*, for example has 559), many events, and an avalanche of detail to immerse the reader in the fabric of the work. Though the novel was dominant, other genres also existed, including in particular the short story. While Turgenev, Dostoevsky, and Tolstoy are most famous for their novels, each did work with the short story, as well as other genres, though to a much lesser extent. And while Garshin made important contributions to the short-story form, he had to deal with the influence of the literary giants of the day as well as with the tradition of the short story as it had developed by the late 1870s.

II *Ivan Turgenev*

The influence of Ivan Turgenev on Vsevolod Garshin is not the sort in which one author borrows from another, but rather the influence of a tradition established by a well-known writer on an impressionable young writer.[1] Garshin does not mention any of

Turgenev's stories in his letters, though he does speak of a sketch and a novel. The sketch, "Death," was included in *A Hunter's Sketches,* one of Turgenev's best and most famous creations, a collection of episodes dealing, for the most part, with the peasant. Garshin uses the sketch in a student composition as a springboard for presenting his own experience with death, i.e., the death of a friend.[2] The novel he refers to is *Virgin Soil,* which he praises. (Fortunately Garshin was a better writer than critic.) Though he does not mention specific short stories by Turgenev, he obviously was familiar with the latter's work. In a letter dated September 8, 1872, for example, he reports having bought an eight-volume edition of Turgenev's works.[3]

Turgenev is best known for his novels and for *A Hunter's Sketches,* but his short stories have come with each succeeding generation to be more and more respected, for they show a variety and an originality he did not always display.[4]

Though the Turgenevian short story is varied in content and in theme, in structure most of the stories follow a regular pattern. His stories usually have a standard opening. The beginning lines may be designed to attract the reader's immediate attention: "It happened in St. Petersburg, in the winter, on the first day of the carnival" ("Yakov Pasynkov"); "The doctor has just left me. At last I have got at something definite!" ("The Diary of a Superfluous Man"). Or else the opening lines may be an introduction in the present to events which have occurred many years before: "Fifteen years ago—began H.—official duties compelled me to spend a few days in the principal town of the province of T***" ("A Strange Story"); "About thirty miles from our village there lived, many years ago, a distant cousin of my mother's, a retired officer of the Guards, and rather wealthy landowner, Alexey Sergeich Telegin" ("Old Portraits"); "At that time I was five-and-twenty, began N.N.,—it was in days long past, as you perceive" ("Asya").

A third type of introduction brings several individuals together, and from their ensuing conversation a story emerges: "In a small, decently furnished room several young men were sitting before the fire" ("Andrey Kolosov"); "We were a party of six, gathered together one winter evening at the house of an old college friend" ("A Lear of the Steppes").[5]

After the opening lines have accomplished their purpose, the structure of the Turgenevian short story follows a particular pattern, which Marina Ledkovsky has defined as follows:

A short exposition at the beginning introduces the reader to the milieu in which the heroes will act, the action develops as the complication (*zavjazka*) of the plot proceeds, then a moment of great tension takes place which is followed by the denouement and frequently by an epilogue indicating in a few words the further destiny of the heroes.[6]

In establishing a standard structure and form for the short story, Turgenev made perhaps one of his greatest contributions to Russian literature. It is of course fruitless to ask whether Alexander Pushkin's "Queen of Spades" or Nikolay Gogol's "The Overcoat" is a better short story than Turgenev's "First Love," for each is great in its own way. Turgenev's achievement lay in creating a corpus of over eighty short stories (including the works in *The Hunter's Sketches*)[7] which solidified the short story as a genre. We occasionally forget the uninterrupted length of Turgenev's writing career. While Dostoevsky's career was interrupted by his Siberian exile and Tolstoy's by his period of nonparticipation in creative literature, Turgenev wrote and published his prose over a period of almost forty years, from "Andrey Kolosov" of 1844 to "Clara Milich" of 1882.

In many ways Garshin rebelled against the Turgenevian short story (about which there is more in the following chapter); in many ways he was influenced by it. Perhaps in dedicating one of his best stories, "The Red Flower," to Turgenev, Garshin was acknowledging this debt. It is interesting to note that Leo Tolstoy also dedicated one of his short stories, "The Wood Felling," to Turgenev.

Like Turgenev, Garshin favors dramatic opening lines to attract the reader, to engage him in some mystery: "The war really gives me no peace" ("The Coward"); " 'Undress!' said the doctor to Nikita, who was standing motionless, his eyes glued to some unknown point in the distance" ("The Orderly and the Officer"); "In the name of his Imperial Majesty and Sovereign Peter the First, I order an inspection of this madhouse" ("The Red Flower").

Or, like Turgenev, Garshin may use the opening to depict a speaker in the present who comments on events in the past: "I remember how we ran through the forest, how the bullets whined, how the branches, broken by the bullets, fell, how we forced our way through the hawthorn bushes" ("Four Days"); "I cannot understand how it has happened that I, not having thought about anything for two years, have begun to think" ("An Occurrence").

Garshin does not employ Turgenev's static opening with individuals in a room conversing, but he does use a universal static opening—that of the fairy tale: "There lived in the world a rose and a toad" ("The Tale of a Toad and a Rose"); "Once upon a time there lived in the world a frog who liked to croak" ("The Frog Traveler").

Garshin next presents the hero and situates him in a particular environment. The opening belongs to the hero, and it is the foil, in Garshin, who invariably intrudes into his world. In Garshin's stories the action then develops as a result of the clash between hero and foil, and while his works often lack the kinds of tension present in Turgenev's stories, he does owe Turgenev a thematic debt in the formation of his conclusions.

Two themes dominate in Turgenev's stories—love and death. These same two themes are prominent in Garshin's stories, especially death. If the opening is the domain of the hero, the ending is usually the realm of the foil, who is a connector to death. Critics have viewed Garshin's works as pessimistic,[8] thanks in part to their final scenes which "end, more or less, with profound sorrow; if not with death, then at least with lifelessness."[9] Scholars have commented on the "overly gory denouement,"[10] the "eighteen deaths in an equal number of works,"[11] the "motif of melancholy disappointment, which so often concludes Garshin's stories."[12]

These critics' observations are certainly valid. Since the conclusion is dominated by the foil and since the foil is invariably connected to death, it follows that death (along with its concomitant grief) is dominant in the denouement of almost every story. In some works it is the foil who dies: "Four Days,"[13] "An Occurrence," "Nadezhda Nikolaevna." In other stories it is the hero who loses his life: "Attalea princeps," "The Tale of a Toad and a Rose," "A Night." Sometimes both the hero and the foil die: "The Coward," "The Red Flower," "The Orderly and the Officer."[14]

The theme of death is so prevalent in the stories of Turgenev and Garshin as to compel us to examine the reasons for its frequent occurrence. The Turgenevian scholar Eva Kagan-Kans sees death in Turgenev as something which can be overcome by forces greater than death, so that it is not an ultimate end but rather an obstacle. "It was not the problem of good and evil, the focal idea of Dostoevsky that interested Turgenev," she writes. "What he probed was the possibility of another existence, beyond the borders of our empirical reality, which would deny the definitiveness of death."[15]

One way to negate the "definitiveness of death" is, of course,

through love, and love in Turgenev's fiction (as in his life) is a force
which enables man to endure, to triumph, to overcome all obstacles,
including death.

In dealing with Garshin's stories we must ascertain why death is
so prevalent in them. Are the endings a manifestation of an authorial
Weltschmerz so powerful it eventually drove Garshin to his own
death? Is death a literary device for dramatically ending a work or
providing a degree of finality to a story? Did the author really intend
to have each story inexorably end with anguish, grief, death, or
hopelessness? Is death inexorably tied to grief and suffering, or is
it, in Garshin as in Turgenev, not an end but a continuation?

In "The Tale of a Toad and a Rose," for example, the rose dies,
but her death brings a smile to the young boy's face. Instead of a
normal life of three days, the rose survives, in a book, for many
years. In "An Occurrence" Nadezhda Nikolaevna refuses to relinquish her life of prostitution and repeatedly rebuffs Ivan Ivanovich.
In the conclusion, though, her reactions when she realizes that he
intends to shot himself is to cry out: "Lord, don't let him do it!
Lord, leave him for me!" (31). Thus she has been deeply affected
by Ivan Ivanovich's love; she now would be willing to forsake her
former life. She shows the reader, finally, that she is capable of
feeling and emotion, that she is a human being and not merely a
"safety valve" of society.

In Garshin's use of the short-story form, in his use of the themes
of love and death, in his use of certain literary techniques, Turgenev
saw, if not his own influence, at least the work of a kindred soul.
In a letter of July 31, 1882, to a friend, the translator Emile Duran,
he expresses the opinion that "Garchine est de tous les jeunes
écrivains russes celui dont le talent fait naître le plus d'espérances."[16]

In a subsequent letter to Garshin, on August 15, 1882, he wrote
more specifically about his work:

I can only repeat to you what, I believe, I wrote to your mother: of all our
young writers, you are the one who arouses the greatest hope. You have
all the qualities of a really great talent: artistic temperament, a fine and
true understanding of the *characteristic*[17] features of life—both human and
general, a sense of truth and measure, simplicity and beauty of form and—
as a result of all this—originality.[18]

Of course the "characteristic features" which Turgenev singles
out in Garshin's stories—truth, measure, simplicity, beauty of

form—are the very qualities which are so prominent in Turgenev's own work. Like Turgenev, Garshin tended toward lyrical prose in describing events and characters, though he avoided the dossierlike biographies and the amount of detail that Turgenev favored. Both writers were precise in their presentations; both showed a marked propensity to use specific examples from the plant and animal kingdoms in creating settings. In evaluating Garshin's writing ability, the master, Turgenev, undoubtedly saw something of himself and was pleased.

In our comparison of Turgenev and Garshin, we should add one further point: in the way he perceived his fellow man, Garshin was similar to Turgenev. Both writers recognized a stark duality in man. Turgenev articulated his view in a famous essay entitled "Hamlet and Don Quixote," in which he discussed the opposing forces and ideas represented by each of these two literary types. Hamlet and Don Quixote are antipodes in psychological makeup, in their goals, in the way each relates or fails to relate to his fellow man. Hamlet is an egotist, a self-centered, self-analyzing, faithless, doubting individual without ideals. Brooding, melancholy, endlessly pondering and reflecting, Hamlet is a centripetal character who cannot establish meaningful contact with others and thus turns ever inward into himself. Don Quixote, in contrast, is a centrifugal character who is concerned with others. He is highly motivated, sure of his dream, happy and enthusiastic in spite of his failures; ruled by his ideal, tempered by his humor, Don Quixote acts while Hamlet, bothered by doubt and reflection, cannot.

Garshin also saw the world dualistically, and life as a conflict of opposing forces. In a letter of 1883 he wrote: "All the people whom I have known are divided (among the divisions there are many, such as: clever people and fools, Hamlets and Don Quixotes, lazy people and active ones, and others) into two categories, or more appropriately, are distributed between two extremes: some are good, but others are bad."[19] In his literary creations Garshin's dualistic outlook was manifested in his use of the hero-foil antipodal relationships.

III   *Leo Tolstoy*

When Garshin, in one of his more unstable periods, visited Tolstoy at his estate, Yasnaya Polyana, in the spring of 1880, Tolstoy was totally unfamiliar with Garshin and his work. By the summer of that year, though, he had come to know at least one of Garshin's

stories, "The Orderly and the Officer," which he valued highly.
Turgenev wrote to Garshin that he, Garshin, occupied "the first
place among beginning young writers. And Count L. N. Tolstoy,
whom I gave to read 'People and War,' shares this opinion."[20]

During this period—the late 1870s and early 1880s—while Garshin was publishing his early stories, Tolstoy had abandoned the
short-story genre in favor of a novel and religious tracts. The final
installment of *Anna Karenina* had appeared in 1877; the religious
tracts—*A Confession, A Criticism of Dogmatic Theology, A Translation and Harmony of the Four Gospels, What I Believe*—were
written during the early 1880s.

In the latter half of the 1880s Tolstoy returned to the short-story
form, though now his works were didactic in nature: "What Men
Live By" (1885), "Where Love Is God Is" (1885), "The Death of
Ivan Ilych" (1886), "How Much Land Does a Man Need?" (1886).

The nature of Tolstoy's unorthodox religious writings in an or-
thodox country precluded their wide dissemination, with the result
that few, including Garshin, were influenced by them during the
decade in which they appeared.

Tolstoy's belles-lettres, on the other hand, were popular and
influential. We may distinguish two chief areas of Tolstoyan influence on Garshin: the military tales and the didactic stories.

Leo Tolstoy and Vsevolod Garshin had similar military experiences: each served during his early twenties in rather exotic places,
Tolstoy in the Caucasus, in Silistria, in the Crimea, Garshin in
Bulgaria; each thought of making the military a career but ultimately
resigned from the service; each was philosophically troubled by the
nature and ultimate purpose of war; each used his firsthand experiences of military action and of military life in his literary work.

Tolstoy published several important military stories: "The Raid"
(1853), "The Wood Felling" (1855), 'Sevastopol in December"
(1855), "Sevastopol in May" (1855), "Sevastopol in August" (1856).[21]
Garshin learned from these stories certain literary techniques which
he would utilize in his own military tales.

Reginald F. Christian, a noted Tolstoy scholar, makes a perceptive observation on Tolstoy's military works when he writes: "Unlike
'Boyhood' and 'Youth' and 'A Landowner's Morning,' Tolstoy's early
military sketches have claimed the attention and won the affection
of his readers, for while they were equally close to him, they show
more attempt on his part to distance himself, to generalise his

experience and to cast it into a literary mould."[22] Garshin employs this same technique. The nameless heroes of "The Coward" and "The Action at Ayaslar," and the Ivanov-heroes of "Four Days" and "From the Reminiscences of Private Ivanov," are typified and generalized. Garshin, like Tolstoy, accomplishes this by his use of a narrator. In both "The Raid" and "The Wood-Felling" "the story is told in the first person by a narrator playing the role more of an observer than of a participant."[23] This is true in those of Garshin's military works which employ the Ich-Erzählung form: "Four Days" and "From the Reminiscences of Private Ivanov." "The Action at Ayaslar" is similar, though it uses a third-person-plural narrator.

In his military stories, Garshin (following Tolstoy's example) concentrates on the sharpness of detail presented through the eyes of a detached observer. Objects and settings are perceived with special clarity which is accomplished by discarding a romanticized or stylized presentation in favor of a specificity of spacial and temporal detail, usually communicated by an observant narrator who is participating in the action:[24] "The troops were to start at ten in the evening. At eight thirty I mounted and rode to the general's . . . " ("The Raid"); "To the right one could see the steep bank of a winding stream and the high wooden posts of a Tartar cemetery; to the left and in front a black strip was visible through the fog" ("The Wood Felling"); "On the North side of the Roadstead, toward noon, two sailors were standing on the telegraph hill between Inkerman and the Northern entrenchment: one of them, an officer, was looking through the telescope fixed there" ("Sevastopol in May").

The following quotation from "The Action at Ayaslar" is an excellent example of Garshin's use of this device: "To the right was a valley along which we had just come, with a stream in the middle and with endless fields of corn, barley and wheat along its slopes. To the left, perpendicular to our valley, was the valley of Lom, fading away on either side into a misty bluish distance . . . " (388–89). A further example of this technique is evident in the opening lines of "From the Reminiscences of Private Ivanov."

Tolstoy often uses inner monologue in his descriptions. In an excellent article entitled "Monologue Intérieur: The Origins of the Formula and the First Statement of Its Possibilities"[25] by the well-known Russian literary scholar Gleb Struve, there is a discussion of inner monologue and its origins. Struve writes that Tolstoy "was probably the first major European writer to make a conscious and extensive use of it."²⁶ Tolstoy employes the device most frequently in *The Sevastopol Stories* and it is probably through these stories that Garshin discovered it.

Garshin figures in an interesting footnote to the discussion on which writer first utilized inner monologue. Edouard Dujardin, a French novelist, claimed to have invented the device and to have been the first to use it in his novel *Les Lauriers sont coupés*.²⁷ He defended his claim to the innovation in a book of 1931, *Le Monologue intérieur: Son apparition, ses origines, sa place dans l'oeuvre de James Joyce*.²⁸ In an article dealing with Dujardin's claim, the literary critic C. D. King defends Dujardin's claim, adding that the writer closest to Dujardin was Vsevolod Garshin, who employed inner monologue in "Four Days." King states:

> But although Garshin did not use his version of inner monologue purely as an end in itself, it must be allowed that he used something very like Dujardin's technique, before *Les Lauriers sont Coupés*. There can, however, be no question of "influence." Had Dujardin known "Four Days" at all, he would surely have mentioned it in *Le Monologue Intérieur;* "Four Days" was translated into French in 1887 by N. V. A. Kolbert, while Dujardin's novel was written between April 1886 and April 1887 and appeared in the *Revue Indépendante* from May to August 1887.²⁹

As to King's first point, there is no guarantee that Dujardin would "surely have mentioned it in *Le Monologue Intérieur*," especially since he claimed to have been the first to use it. Second, both King (p. 124) and Struve (p. 1109), are mistaken in saying that "Four Days" was translated into French in 1887. Actually it first appeared in French translation under the title "Après la Bataille" in 1884.³⁰ In addition Garshin's story "A Night," which also contains some examples of inner monologue, had appeared in French translation in 1882.

All this is not to say that Garshin first used inner monologue. He didn't. We agree with Struve that Tolstoy was probably the first major writer to use the device. Our point is, however, that Garshin was influenced in this area by Tolstoy.

Indeed, in his reminiscences Fausek speaks of the extent of Tolstoy's general influence on Garshin as follows: "The human life portrayed in Tolstoy's novels was for Garshin seemingly more real, more sincere than real life. . . . He reread him dozens of times and remembered every detail. In conversations he often talked about the heroes and varied events from Tolstoy's works as though they were not invention, but actual people, true events."[31]

Garshin's military stories, like Tolstoy's, were immensely popular, because, for the most part, they attracted an audience fervently caught up with the contemporary military situation. The Crimean War and the Russo-Turkish War had the support of the populace, at least in the beginning. In delineating his military characters, Garshin followed Tolstoy in disregarding plot in order to generalize on characters and events. Boris Eikhenbaum, in talking about Tolstoy, could just as well be speaking of Garshin: "His figures are extremely individual, which in the artistic sense means that they are not really personalities, but only the bearers of separate human qualities and features which for the most part are combined paradoxically. These personalities are fluid, the borders between them are not sharply drawn, but the concrete details stand out sharply."[32]

While the above techniques are present in the military stories of each author, they are lacking in the didactic tales, where the stress is neither on plot, nor character development, nor technique, but on moral teaching.[33]

In the didactic tales of both authors, the emphasis is on a straightforward presentation of characters and events culminating in a conclusion containing a moral lesson. The didactic tales are third-person narratives with obvious and clearcut oppositions—good-bad, love-hate, goodness-evil, life-death. The protagonist in the didactic tale usually moves, in the course of the story, from the negative to the positive side as a result of his experiences. Thus in Garshin, King Aggey forever forsakes power as a ruler in order to lead twelve blind men; Vasily Stepanich, as a result of the unselfishness and heroism of Semyon Ivanov ("The Signal"), sees the error of his ways and confesses to his crime, thereby accepting salvation through punishment.

Tolstoy's heroes are often transformed, too. Ivan Ilych ("The Death of Ivan Ilych") and Vasily Brekhunov ("Master and Man") are both arrogant, unfeeling, self-satisfied, tyrannical men; yet each faces death serenely in the end when he recognizes his faults and begins to think of others. Martin Avdeich ("Where Love Is God Is") changes his ways and helps others instead of thinking only of himself, and is rewarded accordingly. When the hero does not learn a lesson, death is often the result, as Pahom discovers in "How Much Land Does a Man Need."

In 1884 Tolstoy (with his friends Vladimir Chertkov and Pavel

Biryukov) founded "Posrednik," a publishing house designed to publish works accessible to the masses. "Posrednik" published Tolstoy's tales for the people plus tales of other writers whose stories were similar in style, content, and manner to Tolstoy's own. Garshin was one such writer. For "Posrednik" he reworked "Four Days," "The Bears," and "The Signal." For his debut in "Posrednik," however, he chose "The Legend of Proud Aggey," the tale which in purpose, in genre, in style, and in content conforms most completely to Tolstoy's principles.

IV Fedor Dostoevsky

The comments in Garshin's letters on Turgenev and Tolstoy are positive, but his comments on Dostoevsky both as man and writer are quite negative. In 1882, for example, Garshin received a letter from his mother in which she discussed allegations on Dostoevsky's moral character made by Gleb Uspensky, a contemporary critic. Garshin wrote back to her that unless there was evidence to the contrary the allegations were probably true, closing the letter with: "you yourself wrote not long ago that Dostoevsky was, by rumor, a detestable person."[34]

A year and a half later Garshin wrote to Vladimir Latkin: "The first volume of Dostoevsky containing his letters has come out . . . If I were to write such trash and then see it in print, I would, to tell the truth, hang myself."[35] Professions of dislike do not preclude literary influence, however, and in several of Garshin's stories— especially "An Occurrence," "A Night," "Nadezhda Nikolaevna," and "Ochen' korotenkii roman," (A Very Short Romance, 1878)— Dostoevsky's influence is apparent. For one thing, Dostoevsky and Garshin frequently described the same types of individuals: prostitutes, alienated city-dwellers, the humiliated and suffering, the suicidal, the arrogant, the morally smug, and the buffoon, among others.

In his first story with an apparent Dostoevskian influence, "An Occurrence," Garshin even acknowledges his debt. He wrote his mother on February 19, 1878, concerning the story and the staff of *Otechestvennye zapiski:* "I don't know for sure whether they will publish it or not. They want everything to be 'intelligent,' but my story is not at all intelligent, but rather 'unintelligible.' Something out of Dostoevshchina. It seems I am inclined toward and capable of following in [Dostoevsky's] footsteps."[36]

"An Occurrence" is, in fact, greatly influenced by *Notes from the Underground*, Dostoevsky's brilliantly original novella of 1864 which served as prologue to the major novels. The influence of this work on Garshin's is evident in character portrayal, in style, in literary technique, and in theme. Garshin's protagonist, like Dostoevsky's, is a contradictory, self-debasing, self-lacerating individual who refuses proffered love out of a fear of (or desire for) pain. Each scorns society and the world at large while taking solace in his isolation and withdrawal to his metaphorical underground. Each, as a result of his education, feels intellectually superior to those around him, and each rationalizes his decision to eschew love, honesty, and compassion by concluding that to accept them would be still worse than rejecting them. Each, instead, experiences the same hurt-and-be-hurt cycle, and each is able to act only in master-slave or slave-master relationships.

Following Dostoevsky's example, Garshin reverses the chronological presentation so that the protagonist and the reader look back to the past, from the vantage point of the present. Thus effect precedes cause. Similar to Dostoevsky's work in manner of presentation, Garshin's, however, lacks the depth of experience and profundity of thought of the great novelist's story.

The Nadezhda Nikolaevna portrayed in "An Occurrence" recalls not only Dosteovsky's man from underground, but also his "infernal" women—Nastasya Filipovna *(The Idiot)*, Grushenka *(The Brothers Karamazov)*, while the Nadezhda of "Nadezhda Nikolaevna" has been altered in character so that she is more reminiscent of the meek, humble Dostoevskian prostitute—Sonya Marmaladova *(Crime and Punishment)* and Liza *(Notes from the Underground)*.

In addition to similarities in female character portrayal and the theme of prostitution, "An Occurrence" and "Nadezhda Nikolaevna" are linked to Dosteovsky through the male characters as well, and through the settings in which these characters act. The love triangle of Nadezhda, Lopatin, and Bessonov finds a parallel to Nastasya Filipovna, Prince Myshkin, and Rogozhin in *The Idiot*. The two males in each work are easily comparable: humble, meek, kind, simple Prince Myshkin is certainly a literary relative to the equally unprepossessing, incorruptible Lopatin; volatile, demonic, unpredictable Rogozhin has a counterpart in Bessonov.

Garshin also draws upon Dostoevsky for the comic relief he inserts into his work. His hunchback Gelfreykh has much in common with Dostoevsky's Lebedev, though their similarity is limited to their superficial buffoonery. Garshin's hunchback certainly lacks the dark, complex nature of Dostoevsky's buffoon. The resolution of the action in "Nadezhda Nikolaevna" also recalls *The Idiot* with the murder of the heroine by the jealous rival and the hero's debilitating illness.

Garshin's "A Night" displays the influence of Dostoevsky, too. The hero of this tale is a tormented, solitary individual who lacerates himself with thoughts of his own worthlessness. Garshin's Aleksey Petrovich, like Dostoevsky's underground man, castigates himself for the pride and filth in his soul. Each sees the falsehood, the sham, the base, the vain in society, and each feels honest and self-righteous as a result of recognizing these traits in himself. Each takes a certain degree of pleasure in privately unburdening his soul through self-mocking, self-denigrating tirades. The result, at least for Aleksey Petrovich, is cathartic: he dies cleansed and happy.

Aleksey Petrovich, like the hero of Dostoevsky's "The Dream of a Ridiculous Man," sees a star as he contemplates suicide. While neither actually does commit suicide, Aleksey Petrovich declines to take this route after he comes to a realization which is decidedly Tolstoyan in nature. His view of his life and of his impending death changes after he reads in the Bible the phrase "Except ye become as little children." He then realizes that one must live for others, that one must not always put oneself first in all things.

A final comparison of Dostoevsky and Garshin might involve "White Nights" and "A Very Short Romance." Garshin's story is a first-person account in which the narrator first informs the reader that he possesses a wooden leg, and then proceeds to tell how he came by his artificial limb. He had fallen in love with a girl, Masha, less than a year before. His Masha "orders" him to fight in the war because "honorable people prove their words by deeds" (401), and promises to become his wife when he returns. By the time he gets back, now without a leg, she is engaged to another. The narrator serves as best man at her wedding, and asks of the reader whether he would "prefer the unhappiness of three people to the unhappiness of one" (403).

The two stories are similar in setting—a white, snowy St. Petersburg night—and tone, with narrative asides and direct questions to the reader. The heroes of both stories are lonely dreamers who wander the streets of St. Petersburg looking timidly for love. In each work the hero finds "love" on a spring night; in each case the woman he encounters lives with a grandmother to whom she reads nightly. The unassertive heroes in each instance lose their love to another, and each bears his grief stoically, refusing to trouble or avenge himself on the woman he loves. Garshin's hero even revels in his martyrdom while serving as best man at her wedding: "I proudly performed my duties during the ceremony, at which time I gave to another that which I valued above all else" (403).

In each case the hero relates past events to the reader in a first-person narrative. Each work is sentimental and ironic, as witnessed by its title ("White Nights: A Tale of Love from the Reminiscences of a Dreamer," "A Very Short Romance"), in setting, in character presentation, and in situation. In Dostoevsky's story irony is a sub-theme, but in Garshin's it is pervasive. Dostoevsky had published his creation in *Otechestvennye zapiski*, a serious journal, signed with his own name. Garshin's tale, on the contrary, appeared in *Strekoza* (Dragon-Fly), a popular humor magazine, signed with the pseudonym *L'homme qui pleure*.

Ultimately Dostoevsky's influence on Garshin was one of setting and technique utilized in several works rather than a philosophical one.

Writing as he did in the shadow of contemporary literary giants, Garshin learned from each, and while he did much to develop and transform the Russian short story, he also was influenced by the tradition of Russian prose. Garshin looked to his masters and took from them ideas on style, structure, and technique.[37] He borrowed from them, to be sure, but adapted his borrowings to fit his own personal literary needs. Thus, though his stories are influenced by the traditional Russian short story, they are nevertheless unique in their own right, and in many ways they signified a break with received tradition. Through the late 1880s and 1890s, Anton Chekhov revolutionized the short story as a genre, but Garshin, in several respects, was a forerunner of this literary revolution.

CHAPTER 9

Garshin and Chekhov

I Introduction

THE decades during which Garshin wrote and published his works witnessed dramatic changes in Russia. These changes were manifested most conspicuously in the industrialization and urbanization of the country. Production of coal, for example, increased from 763,200 tons in 1870 to 3,610,800 in 1880 to 5,049,600 in 1890; oil, from 32,400 tons to 612,200 to 4,348,000.[1] The first Russian census, taken in 1897, showed a total population of 125,-640,000, of which number 16,785,212 lived in towns and cities as compared with only 8,157,000 in 1867.[2]

While many more people were engaged in agriculture than in industry, in terms of total output industry was as important to the nation as agriculture. "By 1900 the aggregate output of Russian industry, which did not occupy more than 10 percent of the population, exceeded in value the output of agriculture, which engaged at least eight times as many persons," writes historian Warren Walsh.[3]

As Russia changed from an agrarian to an industrial country, other concomitant changes occurred: on the one hand there arose a burgeoning proletariat composed, for the most part, of peasants who, unable to survive on the land as a result of the land reform established under Alexander II, moved to the cities; on the other hand the nobility, long provided for by their estates, now had to fend for themselves, and many were compelled to accept jobs for which they were ill-prepared.

Thus life changed drastically for all segments of society, especially those living in the cities. As society changed, so did the literature depicting this society. In the Russia of the late 1880s, Marc Slonim

116

has written, "moral prostration and apathy pervaded educated society; Russia seemed to have resigned itself to the rule of a narrow-
minded bureaucracy, to conformism, to mediocrity."[4]

A writer arose during this era to depict these attributes of Russian
society, a writer who would attain international stature and revo-
lutionize the short-story genre, a writer who would employ many
of Vsevolod Garshin's literary innovations—Anton Chekhov.

II *Antosha Chekhonte*

Both Garshin and Chekhov were admired in their lifetimes as
popular writers of fine short stories, though each followed a different
path. Garshin's second published work, "Four Days," appeared in
one of the major journals and brought its author immediate fame,
partly because of its connection to the Russo-Turkish War, but more
because of its excellence as a creative work of art. Thus at twenty-
two Vsevolod Garshin became a well-known writer in literary Russia.

Chekhov's path to fame was longer and more tortuous. His earliest
stories were humorous anecdotes published in the popular, though
not prestigious, humor magazines of the day, such as *Strekoza.*
Between 1880 and 1882 he published over sixty such anecdotes.
Later in life, when he assembled stories for a multi-volume edition
of his works, he chose to exclude these early creations, feeling, with
some justification, that they had little literary merit.

As his writing and confidence improved (1882–1885) and as he
strove to support his family, Chekhov began publishing large numbers of stories (over one hundred in each of the years 1883 and
1884) in more highly regarded journals, notably *Oskolki* (Frag-
ments), edited by Nikolay Leykin, St. Petersburg's most popular
humor magazine. Many of the stories published in this periodical—
"The Death of a Government Clerk," "The Chameleon," "Sur-
gery"—show that a lively, talented writer was making his presence
felt, though he still signed them with such pseudonyms as "My
Brother's Brother," "Man without a Spleen," and, more commonly,
"Antosha Chekhonte," a nickname from Anton's high school days.

The next year marked a turning point in Chekhov's life as a writer.
The five years he had spent writing humorous works for the popular
journals had been a fertile training ground for developing a certain
approach to the short story. Works published in *Oskolki,* for ex-

ample, in addition to being humorous, also had to be one hundred lines or less in length. Thus in his very early period Chekhov learned to be concise. These early works often dealt with stereotypes portrayed without development or psychological motivation. They were short "moments" stressing caricature over characterization, and usually building toward an unexpected conclusion. In these stories Chekhov depicted with wit and irony the failings and foibles of all levels of society.

In 1885 Anton Chekhov began publishing in two new periodicals—*Peterburgskaya gazeta* (St. Petersburg Gazette, edited by Sergey Khudekov) and *Novoe vremya* (New Time, edited by Aleksey Suvorin). Released now from limitations of length and theme, Chekhov's stories show a maturation of technique and a shift in orientation: impressionistically presented characters replace stereotypes, atmosphere supplants humor, and the emphasis on the conclusion gives way to a concern for inner tension. Encouraged by his new freedom of expression and by a letter from one of the grand old men of Russian letters, Dmitry Grigorovich, exhorting him to take his talent and his stories seriously, Chekhov began reworking his stories into polished form and signing them Anton Chekhov.

By 1888 Chekhov had reached his final plateau. His apprenticeship as a writer, evidenced by his successive journey up the rungs of the ladder of literary success, ended in that year with the appearance of "Step' " (The Steppe) in *Severny vestnik* (Northern Gazette, edited by Aleksey Pleshcheev), one of the "thick journals," as the serious literary reviews of the day were known.

III *Chekhov and Garshin as Writers*

Significantly, of all the stories Chekhov published during Garshin's lifetime, Garshin comments specifically on only one, "The Steppe." Fausek relates how Garshin had visited him at 8:00 A.M. to tell him that "a new, first-class writer has appeared in Russia": Chekhov.[5] Fausek then explains why Garshin made this comment: "He was speaking about 'The Steppe,' a story by Mr. Chekhov which had just appeared in *Severny vestnik*. He had been acquainted with Chekhov's stories since they had started to appear in *Novoe vremya* and valued his talent highly. He had read 'The Steppe' the night before and it produced an extraordinary impression on him."[6]

It is not surprising that Garshin was impressed with "The Steppe" since it has much in common with one of Garshin's own stories, "From the Reminiscences of Private Ivanov": both are long, actionless, plotless works which employ impressionistic devices and seek to create moods, especially through the use of nature.

"The Steppe," subtitled "The Story of a Journey," relates the adventures of nine-year-old Egorushka as he travels across the vast Russian steppe. Egorushka is on his way to school, though he understands neither where he is going nor why. He travels part of the way with his uncle, Ivan Ivanych Kuzmichov, and Father Khristofor Siriysky, who have reluctantly agreed to take him to his school while they are on their way to sell wool to a mysterious, wealthy merchant, Varlamov. For part of the journey, Kuzmichov leaves Egorushka in the care of the peasants who are carting his wool. Whether traveling with his uncle and Father Siriysky or with the peasants, Egorushka "experiences" the steppe. The "plot" of the story consists of a stringing together of experiences related to or witnessed by Egorushka: his hearing a woman's song in the steppe, his encounter with the boy "Tit," a present from Moysey Moyseich's wife, his kiss from the Countess Dranitskaya, the strange appearance of Konstantin, a violent storm, the "ghost" stories around the fire with the peasants, his ultimate abandonment at Nastasya Petrovna's, etc. Rather than forming a true plot, these events exist, instead, as separate isolated episodes and are loosely tied together only by the fact that they occur while Egorushka is present.[7]

The structure in "The Steppe"—a character on a journey participating in a series of events which seemingly have little relevance to a central story line—is similar to the structure employed by Garshin in "From the Reminiscences of Private Ivanov." Garshin's story has much in common with "The Steppe." In both stories, for example, the hero commences his journey across the steppe by passing a cemetery. Garshin's hero imagines the cemetery asking him why he insists on traveling thousands of versts to die when he can die peacefully on his native soil. Egorushka thinks as he passes a cemetery of his grandmother buried there. Since he has just barely begun his journey and is still caught up physically and emotionally in his village and his past, his musings are not melancholy but lovingly reminiscent: "Until her death she was always so alive and would bring soft pretzels sprinkled with poppy seed from the market; now she is sleeping, sleeping. . . ."[8]

Both Ivanov and Egorushka are novices who, dropped by fate into a new environment, are introduced to a cruel, complex world which is very different from what each has known previously. In the course of their respective journeys, both characters develop and mature; both learn that life is not always as it appears to be on the surface. Life, like the steppe, is filled with surprises and wears many guises. Thus Ventsel appears to Ivanov to be an understandable character albeit an unlikable one as well; yet in the end he emerges as much more complex. Reality is deceptive because it is complex. Conversely, Varlamov seems to Egorushka to be a profoundly mysterious individual partly because he exists for Egorushka for the greater part of the story as a hearsay figure. When Egorushka sees Varlamov in the flesh, he seems not at all mysterious. He is, instead, an ordinary, smallish man dressed in gray and sitting on a scrawny, ordinary horse.

Both "heroes" come to understand life more fully as a result of their experiences. Ivanov sees the effect of losing half his men on Ventsel; he observes the randomness of war, the complexity of life, the monotony and horror of death. Egorushka's view of life also changes, as may be illustrated by his musings on his deceased grandmother. As he starts his journey, his thoughts of his grandmother evoke pleasant images; near the end of his trip he envisions a different scene. Now he remembers the dull thuds of the earth being thrown on her coffin and imagines his grandmother, alone, awakening, calling for help, fainting from fear, and dying all over again.

Both Garshin and Chekhov involve their heroes with peasants, who when taken individually are secondary characters, but taken collectively represent a primary character. In order to learn more about them, Ivanov chooses to share a tent with five peasants; he refuses an invitation to move into the officers' quarters. His view of the peasants is certainly an idealized one, and Garshin presents them to us in that way. Chekhov's presentation is much more objective. Egorushka is drawn to the fatherly Panteley while he is frightened of Dymov. In both works it is the peasant who has a firm understanding of events, who has the experience with life which the heroes lack.

However, it is not so much the events themselves which are comparable in the two stories, as it is the manner of presentation Garshin and Chekhov use. In both works there is a loosely episodic presentation of the central character's actions, or more exactly, observations, for in the eight chapters of "The Steppe" and nine of "From the Reminiscences of Private Ivanov" it is not so much physical action on the part of the hero which is significant, but his observations and impressions of others. Not much happens to Ivanov personally in the course of his journey (indeed in the battle scene toward which the story builds his unit is held in reserve), but he sees and describes a great deal of the life going on around him, commenting in detail on his observations. From the daily experiences of the common soldier to the sadness of Ventsel's tears, Ivanov is the medium through which the reader is introduced to a larger world. So it is also with Egorushka. More description is provided of the peasants, of Father Khristofor, of Kuzmichov, than of Egorushka and, while he is not the narrator, it is, by and large, from his perspective that the events are presented.

Both works utilize nature to create and to change moods. The heat of the daytime steppe creates an atmosphere of stagnation and suffocation. Egorushka, being carted across a seemingly endless plain, is stifled by the very air around him. The heat exhausts Egorushka physically and mentally and he frequently lies down to rest, a situation which encourages daydreaming. It also adds to the elongation of time so that the trip through the steppe seemingly occurs at a slowed tempo. In the penultimate chapter, a climax of sorts is reached. A change occurs in the steppe and in those people who are now a part of it. The air becomes oppressive, nature becomes apprehensive and languid. The peasants with whom Egorushka is traveling, though previously talkative and lively, are now bored, tired, and argumentative. Suddenly the steppe is overwhelmed by a storm whose sound and visual effects Chekhov describes in minute detail. The ending of the storm coincides with the ending of Egorushka's journey: he is reunited with his uncle and Father Khristofor, who have successfully completed their business and now deposit him at Nastasya Petrovna's.

Garshin also turns to nature to create mood. The narrator describes his dismal introduction to military life in terms of the weather. The gray uniforms, the physical hardships, the monotony, parallel the gray days of incessant rain as the narrator is baptized into the life of a private in the Russian army. Ventsel is also introduced during the rainy period, but his fiery explosions and sadistic beatings of his soldiers take place during the heat wave which follows the rain.[9]

A further structural similarity between the works is the surprise ending. In reading Chekhov's story we expect something pleasant to happen to Egorushka. One feels that the series of bad events which have befallen him—his separation from his uncle and Father Khristofor, his clash with Dymov, his encounter with the terrifying storm, his illness—must end. And our sense of expectation of good luck is nearly fulfilled: Egorushka is reunited with his uncle and Khristofor, who appears to be genuinely concerned about his illness. They put him to bed and watch over his troubled sleep. The next day, however, Egorushka is better, and so is unceremoniously deposited at Nastasya Petrovna's. The final picture is filled with irony—Kuzmichov tells Egorushka that if he does well in school he will not be forsaken, just when he is about to be forsaken at Nastasya Petrovna's; Kuzmichov and Khristofor each give him a ten-kopeck piece after they have made exceptionally good profits on the sale of their wool; death imagery—Khristofor says, "If I die, pray for me,"[10] Egorushka feels in his soul he will never see the old man again, Kuzmichov speaks "as if a corpse were in the room";[11] pathos—Nastasya cries because her visitors won't stay for tea, and, most important, Egorushka is "greeting his new, unknown life with bitter tears."[12] Chekhov in one further sentence asks what Egorushka's life will be like. Thus the boy is neither saved from abandonment nor clothed in hope for the future.

Garshin's ending also surprises us. Ventsel, for all his expressed dislike of the peasants, is deeply affected by the loss of his men. We expect something to happen with Ventsel—either he will be shot in the back by one of his own men or he will cause some irrevocable harm to one of those under his command. Instead we witness his genuine feeling for those same men who have perished.

In both works our expectations are not realized; in both there is lack of resolution. Instead of telling us what happens to Egorushka, Chekhov asks us what his life will be like. Garshin's first-person narrator reports on Ventsel in his closing scene, but we do not know what happens to the narrator himself. Thus in both works it is neither the departure nor the conclusion of the journey which is significant, but the events, or more accurately, the perception of the events which occur en route.

IV   Impressionism in Garshin and Chekhov

We have seen that it is possible to find similarities in specific stories by Chekhov and Garshin. "The Action at Ayaslar," for ex-

ample, with its detailed, realistic portrayal of military life inter-
spersed with the poetry of nature, calls to mind Chekhov's "The
Kiss," written ten years afterward. "Ward No. 6" has much in common with "The Red Flower." Garshin and Chekhov resemble each
other, however, not so much in specific stories as in their use of
common literary techniques and devices and in the similar struc-
turing of their short stories.

One of the principal areas in which Garshin shows an affinity to
Chekhov is that of impressionistic technique. It is especially in this
area that both writers broke new ground and began to depart from
the literary traditions they had inherited. Impressionism, a true art
movement, flourished in the 1870s and 1880s but never developed
into a literary school, i.e., writers used techniques analogous to
those of the Impressionists, but no specific group of writers followed
its tenets as a "school."

In depicting impressions in their prose, these writers moved from
a concern with philosophical, moral, political, and/or social questions to an effort to communicate a new perception of reality. Events
and objects came to be presented subjectively, as they were perceived by the observer. Thus content became subordinate to form,
and plot gave way to technique. Other features of literary Impressionism include the use of selective details and of light and shadow
to highlight the observed perceptions, and, in contrast to selective
details, the vagueness of the total picture.[13]

These techniques abound in the stories of Chekhov's middle and
late period and in Garshin's stories, especially in the tales of insanity
and in the military tales. However, since Impressionism precludes
the didactic in art, Garshin's fairy tales do not use this technique.

In the overall construction of his short stories Garshin is generally
similar to Chekhov. Both writers discarded lengthy formal intro-
ductions in which elaborate settings were presented and/or detailed
character backgrounds were given, in favor of terse openings. Since
their stories are based on inner tension, on internal rather than on
external action, they had less need to present the developing events
in a logical manner. Therefore, the story opening in their work is
not as important as it is, for example, in the traditional stories of
Turgenev.

What is vital to Chekhov and Garshin is the creation, in the core
of the work, of inner tension, of atmosphere, of internal characterization, of subjective impressions of the outer world. It is a critical
commonplace when speaking of Chekhov to mention that little hap-

pens in his stories (as little happens in Garshin's). Chekhov's story "In the Cart," for example, tells of a teacher's, Marya Vasilevna's, trip to town to collect her salary. Little real action takes place—she meets a neighbor, Khanov, she has tea in a tavern, she fords a stream. Similarly, little real action occurs in "The Action at Ayaslar," "Four Days," "From the Reminiscences of Private Ivanov," "A Night," etc.; and yet, so much is communicated to the reader, so much does happen to Marya on her journey. The key is, of course, that Chekhov highlights not actions of a real world, but the thoughts, moods, anxieties, and impressions of a perceived world. The same may be said of Garshin. It is in this new approach that Chekhov and Garshin made their greatest contribution to Russian literature, for it became the basis for the modern short story as it developed in Europe, England, and the United States.

In dealing with the structure of their short stories, we should add that both Garshin and Chekhov, in breaking away from the traditional form of the short story, extended this break to the endings as well. Both found it unnecessary to build up to a climax or denouement in which threads were brought together and events were carried to a logical conclusion. Instead they came to use unexpected or zero endings. [14] The former is a surprise ending—the reader is led to expect a certain outcome but is deceived in that expectation. The less traditional zero ending is also based on a nonrealized expectation. The reader is led to expect a dramatic outcome to the plot which never materializes. Instead there is an inexplicable dissipation of tensions. The disparity between expectation and realization in Chekhov's and Garshin's stories intensifies the inner tension in these works.

We can demonstrate the similarities of technique and structure in the works of the two authors by comparing two stories—"In the Cart" and "The Meeting." Thematically they differ greatly but in the approach each author uses there is much in common. Neither author provides much factual information in the opening, preferring instead to create a mood. Garshin's protagonist, Vasily Petrovich, gazes at a moonlit strip reflected on the broad expanse of the Black Sea. This is the first time he has seen such a sight, and he loses himself in the romanticized landscape. Chekhov's protagonist, Marya Vasilevna, immune to nature's call, is totally unaffected by her surroundings—the woods, the spring sunshine, the black flocks of birds, the blue sky. Instead of giving us data about their char-

acters' pasts, the authors delineate their characters' present states
of mind.

As each author begins to develop the main body of his story, he
introduces another character, Khanov and Kudryashov in "In the
Cart" and "The Meeting," respectively. Their presence contributes
little to the development of any external action. Khanov and Kudryashov are important for the effect they have on the heroes' inner
worlds. Vasily Petrovich observes and forms impressions of Kudryashov as Marya Vasilevna does of Khanov, and these impressions
convey a great deal about those who have formed them. Vasily talks
with Kudryashov, but doesn't really communicate with him; he
cannot reconcile Kudryashov's deeds with his own moral perception
of right and wrong. Marya talks with Khanov, but we learn little
from their conversation. What we do learn about him, we learn
from the impressions she forms of him, of the way he appears to
be to her:

He seemed to be well built, vigorous, but there was something barely
perceptible in his gait which revealed a creature already poisoned, weak,
near his end. And it was as though the forest suddenly smelled of wine.
Marya Vasilevna became frightened and began to pity this man who was
perishing without rhyme or reason and it occurred to her that if she were
his wife or sister, then, it seemed, she could give her whole life in order
to save him.[15]

Both stories emphasize the thoughts, moods, impressions, and
anxieties of their schoolteacher heroes, though both authors often
use objects and images of the physical world (stressing those which
appeal to our sense of sight and smell) as a means of moving from
the outer to the inner world. In addition to the nature settings
already mentioned, we find in Chekhov's story the smell of cologne
and wine attached to Khanov; Marya's photograph of her mother,
which has so faded from dampness that only the hair and eyebrows
are visible; the tavern with its smell of vodka, tobacco, and sheep-
skins. Garshin, in his story, sets off Vasily's mental state from Kudryashov's physical one. The latter is emphasized in the descriptions
of Kudryashov's fancy carriage, his elaborately furnished house, the
huge quantities of fine foods and wines consumed in the course of
the story, and, of course, in the detailed depiction of the aquarium.

Chekhov and Garshin end their stories in a similar manner, i.e.,

with zero endings. We expect something to happen to Marya Vasilevna on her journey, perhaps something dramatic as she fords the
river, certainly something connected with Khanov and Marya's feelings toward him. And, indeed, we are led to this point. As she waits
for a train to pass, she falls to daydreaming of her youth and her
family, at which moment Khanov drives up:

Seeing him she imagined such happiness as had never been, and she smiled
and nodded her head at him as an equal and an intimate, and it seemed
to her that the sky, the trees and all the windows were glowing with her
happiness, her triumph. No, her father and mother had never died, she
had never been a schoolteacher: that was a long, oppressive, strange dream,
but now she had awakened. . . . "[16]

But nothing comes of this dream. It vanishes with the raising of
the barrier. Marya has reached home, the threads of the story
remain untied, and there is no resolution, no ending. In like manner
we expect some event to occur in "The Meeting" to resolve the
dispute between Vasily and Kudryashov. But there is no resolution.
Vasily is stunned by the magnificence of the aquarium; after viewing
it, he and Kudryashov return to the dining room, where another
bottle of wine awaits them. Thus this story also ends with no ending.
Climax is replaced by confusion, and we never learn the outcome
of Vasily's moral dilemma.

V   Chekhov and the Garshinian Collection

Chekhov observed the development of Russian literature closely
from the time he himself began to write, and so was fully aware of
Vsevolod Garshin, the writer. In a letter to Nikolay Leykin of January 1887, Chekhov remarks that of all the writers who had begun
their careers during Chekhov's lifetime, only three are noteworthy:
Vsevolod Garshin, Vladimir Korolenko, and Semyon Nadson.
Though the poet Nadson has not stood the test of time, the prose
writers Korolenko and Garshin have.

By 1887 Chekhov was coming into his own as an author. Though
his best works were still in the future, he had published some fine
stories by this date: "Sergeant Prishibeev," "The Huntsman,"
"Vanka," and many others. Thus his was the praise of one fine
author for another, and when Garshin died a year later, Chekhov

was affected both by Garshin's death and the manner of his death. "It's interesting," he wrote, "that for a week before his death he knew that he would throw himself into the stairwell and prepared for that end. An unbearable life! And the stairs are horrible. I saw them: dark, dirty. . . . "[17]

In 1888 a project was undertaken to honor the deceased writer and to raise funds for a monument by publishing a collection of poems, stories, and articles by various authors. Actually two collections were begun: one, *Krasnyi tsvetok* (The Red Flower), was organized by Kazimir Barantsevich and a group of writers associated with the newspaper *Novosti* (News); the other, *Pamiati V. M. Garshina* (In Memory of V. M. Garshin), was undertaken under the leadership of Aleksey Pleshcheev and a group connected with the journal *Severny vestnik*.

Each group wanted Chekhov's participation. Barantsevich wrote him on March 29, 1888, and Chekhov, not knowing he would be receiving a second, identical request the next day and feeling morally bound as a writer to help honor a colleague, dashed off an affirmative reply asking by what date the story was needed and whether it was possible to contribute a work which had already been published. On the latter point, Chekhov felt that if writers could contribute previously published works, the collection would be of a higher caliber, for each writer would select his or her best work. It is difficult to determine whether Chekhov was truly concerned with the success of Barantsevich's venture or whether he was trying to avoid having to pen a new creation for which he would receive no financial return. Since Chekhov was in a literary slump at the time, especially with short fiction, perhaps he was genuinely fearful of not being able to contribute a new work.

On the following day Chekhov received Pleshcheev's letter requesting a story and begging him not to contribute to the rival undertaking. This put him in an uncomfortable situation. He was closer to Pleshcheev and would have preferred working with him, but he was also an honorable man and could not consider going back on his word to Barantsevich.

For a while it looked as though his problem might be solved for him. Pleshcheev and Barantsevich met and attempted to combine their efforts by publishing one collection jointly honoring Garshin, but they could not reach a mutually satisfactory agreement. This bothered Chekhov, not only because he remained bound to Barantsevich's group, but because he saw the financial foolishness of such a duplicative effort.[18]

As it turned out, Chekhov and Barantsevich never agreed on a story. Chekhov misplaced the one he wanted to include in the collection; Barantsevich rejected the one Chekhov sent in its place and, as a result, the *Novosti* group published their work—*Krasnyi tvetok. Literaturnyi sbornik v pamiat' V. M. Garshina* (The Red Flower. A Literary Collection in Memory of V. M. Garshin)—without anything by Anton Chekhov. Pleshcheev, however, continued to hound Chekhov, asking him to contribute something no matter how small.

Chekhov's reaction to Pleshcheev's repeated requests was the same as to Barantsevich's. He wanted to participate, he wished to honor Garshin's memory, especially since he had taken an interest in him,[19] and he wanted to be included with the other contributors, for his reputation would be damaged if he were not. Though his heart was in the right place, Chekhov could find nothing appropriate for the collection, or so he repeatedly claimed to Pleshcheev. Finally, however, he wrote in a letter of September 15, 1888:

I do have one topic, though: a young man similar in character to Garshin, remarkable, honest and profoundly sensitive, lands, for the first time in his life, in a brothel. As it is necessary to speak seriously about that which is serious, so in this story all things will be called by their real names. . . . Will you guarantee, my friend, that the censor or the editor himself will not take out that which I consider important? . . . If you guarantee that *not one*[20] word will be expunged, then I will write the story in two evenings; if you can't guarantee it, then wait a week and I'll give you my final answer.[21]

Pleshcheev replied with a guarantee that nothing would be censored or changed in the story. But when a month rather than a week passed, Pleshcheev, in despair, wrote Chekhov that he was ruining the project by his procrastination. In desperation Pleshcheev begged him to send a work as he had promised. Chekhov dawdled and delayed a few more days and finally sent off the story on November 13, 1888. It was "Pripadok" (A Nervous Breakdown).[22]

As the protagonist of his story Chekhov chose a hero with characteristics and concerns very similar to Garshin's. The protagonist, Vasilev, is deeply disturbed by various aspects of his experiences with several brothels: the terrible bad taste of the decorations, the openness with which business is carried on, and most of all, by the prostitutes themselves, who, he feels, are no longer real people. He tries to invent solutions for prostitution as a social disease, but is unable to; finally he finds temporary respite in medicines prescribed by a psychiatrist.

The story, dealing as it does with prostitution, an overly sensitive hero, a medical student, and an artist, calls to mind Garshin's "Nadezhda Nikolaevna" and it is apparent why Chekhov wrote this work for Pleshcheev's collection.

VI *Conclusion*

Through Anton Chekhov the Russian short story greatly influenced and altered the modern short story in general. Since many of the techniques Chekhov used were standard elements in Garshin's stories, and since Chekhov published his best and most significant stories after Garshin's death, it is safe to conclude that, in many respects, Garshin was a forerunner of Chekhov in the development of the short story.

Garshin's contemporaries, unfortunately, did not read him for his innovative contributions to the genre; instead they were interested in the themes and purported social messages of his works. The modern reader, on the other hand, is more appreciative of the intrinsic qualities of his stories, more cognizant of his manner of expression. Thus while Garshin pales by comparison with the great writers of his day such as Dostoevsky, Tolstoy, and Turgenev in content, breadth, and diversity, he is frequently their equal in manner and originality of expression.

It is in this area that Garshin's importance in Russian literature lies, then, for in many respects he prepared the way for the modern form of the short story and thus bridged the gap between the prose giants of the pre-1881 era and the emerging great writers of *fin de siècle* Russia. Adolf Stender-Petersen has written: "He brought the *sensitive* short story to its full development and thereby influenced its literary development. With his short story art he would become the forerunner of the great modern Russian short story writers Leskov, Korolenko, Chekhov and Gorky."[23]

To the above list we could also add Leonid Andreev, a fine early-twentieth-century writer and the only writer who publicly acknowledged his indebtedness to Garshin.[24]

When Vsevolod Garshin came on the literary scene in the late 1870s, Russian literature was in a state of flux. The novel was about to yield to other genres. Drama during this period was largely dormant, awaiting Chekhov, Stanislavsky, and the Moscow Art Theater. Semyon Nadson popularized poetry, and even if his poetry could not stand comparison with that of the later Silver Age poets, *Nadsonshchina* captivated a generation and revived poetry as a genre. It was the short story, though, developing through the late 1870s and the 1880s, which supplanted the novel. In his brief literary career Garshin was instrumental in the development and popularization of this genre.

Notes and References

Chapter One

1. Unless otherwise stated, all dates are given old style.
2. V. M. Garshin, *Polnoe sobranie sochinenii. Pis'ma* (Complete Works: Letters) (Moscow: Academia, 1934), III, 12. This volume contains all of Garshin's extant letters. Volumes I and II were to contain his belles-lettres, but these volumes were never published. Henceforth this work will be referred to as Garshin, *Pis'ma*.
3. Garshin, *Pis'ma*, p. 12.
4. E. M. Garshin, "Vospominaniia brata" (Remembrances of a Brother), in V. M. Garshin, *Polnoe sobranie sochinenii* (Complete Works) (St.Petersburg: Marks, 1910), p. 10.
5. Garshin, *Pis'ma*, p. 12.
6. Ibid., p. 413.
7. Ibid., p. 29.
8. Ibid., p. 95.
9. M. Klevenskii, *V. M. Garshin* (Moscow: Gosudarstvennoe izdatel'stvo, 1925), pp. 16–17.
10. Garshin, *Pis'ma*, p. 70.
11. Ibid., p. 116.
12. Ibid., p. 121.
13. Klevenskii, *Garshin*, p. 25.
14. Garshin, *Pis'ma*, p. 160.
15. For a fuller discussion of Garshin's contact with Loris-Melikov, see Garshin, *Pis'ma*, pp. 475–77; for a copy of the letter, see p. 207.
16. For a more detailed account of Garshin's stay, see V. S. Akimov, "Vospominaniia diadi (Remembrances of an Uncle), in V. M. Garshin, *Polnoe sobranie sochinenii* (St. Petersburg: Marks, 1910), pp. 15–20.
17. Garshin, *Pis'ma*, p. 234.
18. Ibid., p. 334.
19. Ibid., p. 358.
20. While the obituary notice (*Severnyi vestnik*, St. Petersburg, April 1888) states that Garshin fell, it is more popularly assumed that his fall was

intentional. See, for example, M. A. Protopopov, "Vsevolod Garshin,"
Literaturno-kriticheskie kharakteristiki (Literary-Critical Characteristics)
(St. Petersburg: B. M. Wolf, 1896), pp. 255–82.

Chapter Two

1. Garshin, *Pis'ma*, pp. 462–63.
2. All quotations are taken from V. M. Garshin, *Sochineniia* (Works)
(Moscow: Gos. Izd. Khudozh. Lit., 1955). Page numbers from this edition
will be enclosed in parentheses in the text. All translations, unless otherwise
noted, are my own.
3. Olga Główko, "Narracja w noweli W. Garszyna 'Cztery dni' " (Narration in V. Garshin's story "Four Days"), *Slavia Orientalis* 3(1973): 318.
4. In addition to the time sequence of four days, a further connection
to the Lazarus story is found in the fact that Lazarus was of Bethany, the
village of Mary (and Martha). The woman mentioned in "Four Days" is
Masha, the diminutive of the Russian equivalent of Mary.
5. Garshin's italics.
6. Turgenev especially liked the story and regretted that the projected
book was never completed. See Garshin, *Pis'ma*, p. 480.
7. George Siegel, "The Art of Vsevolod Garshin," Diss. Harvard University, 1958, Chapter 2, p. 51.
8. This technique is discussed in Chapter 8 in connection with Tolstoy's
influence on Garshin.
9. Garshin's italics.

Chapter Three

1. It is this quotation which particularly annoyed the editors of *Otechestvennye zapiski* and led them to judge the story as too pessimistic.
2. S. V. Shuvalov, "Garshin-khudozhnik" (Garshin—The Artist), in
V. M. Garshin, ed. E. F. Nikitina (Moscow: Kooperativnoe izdat. pisatelei,
1931), p. 112.
3. For an interesting and entertaining definition of this word, see Vladimir Nabokov, *Nikolai Gogol* (New York: New Directions, 1944),
pp. 63–74.
4. A verst (Russian *versta*) is a measure of distance equal to 3,500 feet.
5. Shuvalov, "Garshin-khudozhnik," p. 113.
6. V. A. Fausek, "Vospominaniia" (Remembrances), in V. M. Garshin,
Polnoe sobranie sochinenii (St. Petersburg: Marks, 1910), pp. 48–49.
7. My italics.
8. D. M. Moldavskii, "Nekotorye voprosy fol'klorizma V. M. Garshina."
(Some Questions on V. M. Garshin's Use of Folklore), *Russkii fol'klor:*

Materialy i issledovaniia (Russian Folklore: Materials and Studies) 7 (Moscow: Izdatel'stvo Akademii nauk SSSR, 1962): 132.
9. See note by I. V. Sreznevskii in *Polnoe sobranie sochinenii Tolstogo* (Tolstoy's Complete Works) (Moscow: GIZ, 1929), XI, 460.
10. See note by N. Gudzii in *Polnoe sobranie sochinenii Tolstogo* (Moscow: GIZ, 1936), XXVI, 855–57.
11. Garshin, *Pis'ma,* p. 249.
12. See, for example, Garshin, *Sochineniia,* p. 423.

Chapter Four

1. Garshin's italics.
2. Taking a journey is the same metaphor Dostoevsky uses for suicide, as with Svidrigailov in *Crime and Punishment,* for example.
3. Garshin, *Pis'ma,* p. 154.
4. For some interesting, though at times farfetched, insights into the question of Garshin and art, especially in "Nadezhda Nikolaevna," see Leland Fetzer, "Art and Assassination: Garshin's 'Nadezhda Nikolaevna,' " *Russian Review* 34:1 (1975): 55–65.
5. Karl D. Kramer, "Impressionist Tendencies in the Work of Vsevolod Garshin," *American Contributions to the Seventh International Congress of Slavists,* ed. Victor Terras (The Hague: Mouton, 1973), II, 351.
6. For the complete history of Charlotte Corday, see Alphonse Marie Louis de Lamartine, *Histoire des Girondins* (The History of the Girondists) (Brussels: Meline, Cans et Compagnie, 1848), pp. 642–65.
7. Garshin, *Pis'ma,* p. 228.
8. Bernard Isaacs, in the only English translation of "The Artists" (*The The Scarlet Flower* [Moscow: Foreign Language Publishing House, n.d.]) translates *glukhar'* as "the human anvil." This gives some idea of the physical abuse which the boiler worker must bear, but cannot convey the loss of hearing inherent in this word. Since an exact equivalent does not exist in English, we will use "the human anvil" throughout.
9. *Blednyi* is an epithet frequently used by Garshin to show a strong emotional reaction to an event or person. Laconic in his prose, he often eschews description in favor of set epithets which play an important role in delineating a character's response to an external stimulus.
10. Garshin's italics.
11. Kramer, "Impressionist Tendencies," p. 347.
12. Ibid.
13. Ibid.
14. See, for example, S. Andreevskii, "V. M. Garshin," *Russkaia mysl'* 6 (1889): 55.

Chapter Five

1. M. E. Saltykov-Shchedrin, *Polnoe sobranie sochinenii* (Complete Works) (Moscow: Gos. Izd. Khudozh. Lit., 1939), XIX, 141.
2. I. S. Turgenev, *Polnoe sobranie sochinenii i pisem: Pisma* (Complete Works and Letters: Letters) (Moscow: Nauka, 1960), XIII, Book 2, 27.
3. N. K. Mikhailovskii, "O Vsevolode Garshine" (About Vsevolod Garshin) in *Pamiati V. M. Garshina* (In Memory of V. M. Garshin) (St. Petersburg: Shtein, 1889), p. 164.
4. Ibid., p. 186.
5. Garshin, *Pis'ma*, p. 297.
6. Korney Chukovsky was the first critic to note the schematic nature of the descriptions. See Chukovsky's *Sobranie sochinenii* (Collected Works) (Moscow: Khudozh. Lit., 1969), VI, 426.
7. In Zoroastrianism Ahriman was the spirit of evil. He was opposed to Ormazd, the creator of the world and the embodiment of good.
8. N. Kostomarov, ed., *Pamiatniki starinnoi russkoi literatury* (Monuments of Old Russian Literature) (St. Petersburg: Kulich, 1860), p. 130.
9. My italics.
10. For an excellent study of Garshin's use of narrative voice, see Lennart Stenborg, *Studien zur Erzähltechnik in den Novellen V. M. Garshins* (Studies of Narrative Technique in the Stories of V. M. Garshin), *Studia Slavica Upsaliensis* 11 (Uppsala: University of Uppsala, 1972): 51.
11. See, for example, Andreevskii, "V. M. Garshin," p. 58.

Chapter Six

1. My italics.
2. See, for example, Kramer, "Impressionistic Tendencies," p. 348.
3. Ibid.
4. V. N. Arkhangelskii, "Osnovnoi obraz v tvorchestve Garshina" (The Basic Form in Garshin's Works), *Literatura i marksizm* 2 (1929): 81.
5. Paul Varnai, "The Prose of V. Garshin," Diss. University of Michigan, 1970, p. 76.
6. Garshin even contemplated writing a story with a title like Gogol's, as evidenced by a letter (March 5, 1876) in which he discussed future literary plans: "This summer I'm going to write [the following works:] 'Istoriia progimnazii' [The History of a Gymnasium], 'Povest' o tom, kak possorilis St. Dm. s A. A.' [The Story of How St. Dm. Quarreled with A. A.], 'Intensivnaia kul'tura' [Intensive Culture], 'Istoriia N. obiteli' [The History of the Inhabitants of N]": Garshin, *Pis'ma*, p. 71.
7. Of course even in the third-person narratives, though, he intermixes dialogue, inner monologue, inner voices, etc.

Chapter Seven

1. Mikhailovskii, "O V. Garshine," p. 164.
2. V. Kostrshchitsa, "Deistvitel'nost', otrazhennaia v ispovedi" (Reality Reflected in Confession), *Voprosy literatury* 12 (1966): 139.
3. Ju. Elagin, "V. M. Garshin," *Russkii vestnik* 13 (1891): 284.
4. G. A. Bialyi, *Vsevolod Garshin* (Leningrad: Prosveshchenie, 1969), pp. 75–79.
5. G. A. Bialyi, "Korolenko i novye veianiia v russkom realizme kontsa XIX veka. Garshin, Chekhov." (Korolenko and the New Trends in Russian Realism at the End of the 19th Century. Garshin, Chekhov), in Bialyi, *V. G. Korolenko* (Moscow: Gos. Izd. Khudozh. Lit., 1949), p. 330.
6. Garshin's italics.
7. Garshin's use of inner monologue is discussed below in Chapter 8.
8. Garshin, *Pis'ma*, p. 72.
9. Ibid.
10. Ibid., p. 74.
11. H. Gerigk, "Vsevolod Garshin als Vorläufer des russischen Symbolismus" (Vsevolod Garshin as a Forerunner of Russian Symbolism), *Die Welt der Slaven* 3 (1962): 257.
12. E. M. Forster, *Aspects of the Novel* (New York: Harcourt, Brace and Company, 1927), p. 118.
13. A. M. Skabichevskii, *Istoriia noveishei russkoi literatury* (History of Recent Russian Literature) (St. Petersburg: Obschchestvennaia pol'za, 1903), p. 370.
14. Chukovskii, *Sob. soch.*, VI, 439.
15. For a discussion of the role of description in Garshin's stories, see Varnai, "The Prose of Garshin," pp. 61–87.

Chapter Eight

1. Parallel situations can be found in the stories of both writers. See, for example, Varnai, "The Prose of Garshin," p. 16, where a comparison is developed between "Nadezhda Nikolaevna" and Turgenev's "Diary of a Superfluous Man." Direct literary influence is much more difficult to prove.
2. See *Krasnyi tsvetok. Literaturnyi sbornik v pamiat' V. M. Garshina* (The Red Flower. A Literary Collection in Memory of V. M. Garshin) (St. Petersburg: Skorokhodov, 1889), pp. 6–9.
3. Garshin, *Pis'ma*, p. 435.
4. Two recent works have done much to change the previously accepted view that Turgenev was a not too profound, genteel writer concerned with describing the changing social milieu in his novels: Eva Kagan-Kans, *Hamlet and Don Quixote: Turgenev's Ambivalent Vision* (The Hague: Mouton,

1975); Marina Ledkovsky, *The Other Turgenev: From Romanticism to Symbolism* (Würtzburg: Jal-verlag, 1973).

5. The translations from Turgenev's belles-lettres are taken from *The Novels of Ivan Turgenev*, trans. Constance Garnett (New York: Macmillan Co., 1906), 15 volumes. This third type is similar to a frame-story (*Rahmenerzählung*), which is, of course, an established subgenre of the short story.

6. Ledkovsky, *The Other Turgenev*, p. 31.

7. For a discussion of the classification of *The Hunter's Sketches*, see Dmitry Cizevskij, *History of Nineteenth-Century Russian Literature*, trans. R. Porter (Nashville: Vanderbilt Univ. Press, 1974), II, 29–32.

8. See, for example, Jan Brodal, "The Pessimism of V. M. Garshin," *Scando-Slavica* 19(1973): 17–30.

9. Mikhailovskii, "O Garshine," p. 175.

10. K. K. Arsen'ev, "V. M. Garshin i ego tvorchestvo" (V. M. Garshin and His Works), in Garshin, *Polnoe sobranie sochinenii* (St. Petersburg: Marks, 1910), p. 537.

11. Arkhangel'skii, "Osnovnoi obraz," p. 87.

12. L. A. Iezuitova, "Leonid Andreev i Vs. Garshin," *Vestnik Leningradskogo universiteta: Seriia istorii, iazyka i literatury* 8 (1964): 101.

13. Despite the fact that the Turk dies in the opening, his death there is symbolic. He does not die for Ivanov until the closing, when he has lost his human form.

14. Here death is connected to both in the dreams they have.

15. Eva Kagan-Kans, "Fate and Fantasy: A Study of Turgenev's Fantastic Stories," *Slavic Review* 28 (1969): 546.

16. I. S. Turgenev, *Polnoe sobranie sochinenii i pisem v dvadtsati vos'mi tomakh. Pis'ma.* (Complete Works and Letters in Twenty-Eight Volumes. Letters), XIII, Book 1 (Leningrad: Nauka, 1967), 318.

17. Turgenev's italics.

18. Garshin, *Pis'ma*, p. 496.

19. Ibid., p. 291.

20. Turgenev, *Pol. sob. soch.*, XII, Book 2, 273–74. As noted above, "The Orderly and the Officer" was the first in a series of sketches to be entitled *Liudi i voina* (People and War). The subsequent sketches were never written.

21. In addition to the five listed above, we could also include the lesser-known "Meeting a Moscow Acquaintance in the Detachment" and the quasi-military "The Cossacks." Though we are discussing short stories, Tolstoy also used these techniques in his novels, most notably in *War and Peace*.

22. R. F. Christian, *Tolstoy: A Critical Introduction* (Cambridge: Cambridge Univ. Press, 1969), p. 49.

23. Boris Eikhenbaum, *The Young Tolstoy*, translation edited by Gary Kern (Ann Arbor: Ardis, 1972), p. 82.

24. For a fuller discussion of Tolstoy's use of this technique see Eikhenbaum, *The Young Tolstoy,* pp. 33–39.

25. Gleb Struve, *"Monologue Intérieur:* The Origins of the Formula and the First Statement of Its Possibilities," *PMLA* 69 (December 1954): 1101–11.

26. Struve, *"Monologue Intérieur,* " p. 1110.

27. Edouard Dujardin, *Les Lauriers sont coupés* (The Laurels Are Cut), serialized in 1887; published in book form in Paris: Librairie de la Revue Indépendante, 1888.

28. Edouard Dujardin, *Le Monologue Intérieur: Son apparition, ses origines, sa place dans l'oeuvre de James Joyce* (Interior Monologue: Its Appearance, Origins, and Place in the Works of James Joyce) (Paris: Albert Messein, 1931).

29. C. D. King, "Edouard Dujardin, Inner Monologue and the Stream of Consciousness," *French Studies* 7 (1953): 116–28.

30. "Après la Bataille" (After the Battle), *Revue Bleue,* April 26, 1884.

31. V. A. Fausek, "Vospominaniia," p. 46.

32. Eikhenbaum, *The Young Tolstoy,* p. 34.

33. For a good analysis of the later didactic folk stories see: Gary Jahn, L. N. Tolstoj's Folk Stories [article in English], *Russian Language Journal,* 31 (Spring 1977): 67–78.

34. Garshin, *Pis'ma,* p. 237.

35. Ibid., p. 304.

36. Ibid., p. 156.

37. For studies of Garshin's literary relationship with his great contemporaries, see F. I. Evnin, "F. M. Dostoevskii i V. M. Garshin," *Izvestiia Akademii nauk SSSR: Otdelenie literatury i iazyka* 21:4 (1962): 289–301; D. V. Grishin, "V. Garshin," in *Dnevnik pisatelia F. M. Dostoevskogo* (Melbourne: Melbourne Univ., 1966), pp. 34–37; Robert Louis Jackson, *Dostoevsky's Underground Man in Russian Literature* (The Hague: Mouton, 1958); O. Mirtov, "Voina v proizvedeniiakh Tolstogo, Garshina i Andreeva" (War in the Works of Tolstoy, Garshin and Andreev), *Obrazovanie* 10 (1905): 16–32; Fan Parker, *Vsevolod Garshin: A Study of a Russian Conscience* (Morningside Heights, N.Y.: King's Crown Press, 1946); Paul Varnai, "The Prose of V. Garshin," Diss. University of Michigan, 1970; Ellinor Zelm, *Studien über Vsevolod Garshin* (Studies of Vsevolod Garshin), 1935; rpt. (Nendeln/Liechtenstein: Kraus Reprint, 1968).

Chapter Nine

1. Warren Walsh, *Russia and the Soviet Union* (Ann Arbor: University of Michigan Press, 1958), p. 290.

2. Ronald Hingley, *Russian Writers and Society 1825–1904* (New York: McGraw Hill, 1973), p. 163.

3. Walsh, *Russia and the Soviet Union,* p. 313.

4. Marc Slonim, *From Chekhov to the Revolution* (New York: Oxford University Press, 1962), p. 13.

5. Garshin, *Pis'ma,* p. 523.

6. Ibid.

7. The structure of the story has even been called an antiplot. See Donald Rayfield, *Chekhov: The Evolution of his Art* (New York: Barnes and Noble, 1975), p. 72. For an excellent discussion of the story, especially the role played by Egorushka, see Jerome H. Katsell, "Čexov's *The Steppe* Revisited," *Slavic and East European Journal* 22:3(1978): 313–23.

8. Anton Chekhov, *Polnoe sobranie sochinenii i pisem. Sochineniia* (Complete Works and Letters. Works) (Moscow: Nauka, 1977), VII, 14–15.

9. The narrator, a resident of the steppe, is not bothered as much by the heat as his fellow soldiers, most of whom hail from the north.

10. Chekhov, *Sochineniia,* VII, 104.

11. Ibid.

12. Ibid.

13. For a discussion of literary Impressionism and its relevance to Chekhov, see Dmitri Chizhevsky, "Chekhov in the Development of Russian Literature," in *Chekhov: A Collection of Critical Essays,* ed. Robert Louis Jackson (Englewood Cliffs, N.J.: Prentice-Hall, 1967); Charanne Carroll Clarke, "Aspects of Impressionism in Chekhov's Prose" and Savely Senderovich, "Chekhov and Impressionism: An Attempt at a Systematic Approach to the Problem," in *Chekhov's Art of Writing: A Collection of Critical Essays,* ed. Paul Debreczeny and Thomas Eekman (Columbus, Ohio: Slavica Publishers, Inc., 1977). For a discussion of Garshin and Impressionism, see Kramer, "Impressionistic Tendencies in the Work of Vsevolod Garshin."

14. For a discussion of the zero ending by the originator of the term, see Viktor Shklovskii, *Khod konia* (Knight's move) (Moscow, 1923), pp. 119–20.

15. Chekhov, *Sochineniia,* IX, 338.

16. Ibid., p. 342.

17. Chekhov, *Pis'ma,* II, 230. Chekhov's view that Garshin had planned his death for a week stems, probably, from a letter Chekhov had received from Barantsevich in which the latter related the details of a meeting he had had with Garshin a week before his death. See Chekhov, *Pis'ma,* II, 469.

18. Chekhov, with an eye toward the financial end, writes Pleschcheev: "If my instincts don't deceive me, I am almost certain that the collection issued last will not be successful, that is, it will run aground. Consequently, one must resort to cunning: announce now, while the impression of death is still fresh, a subscription to the proposed collection; announce it and keep announcing it without letup until September": *Pis'ma,* II 232.

19. We have in mind here the interest and admiration Garshin showed for "The Steppe," which had recently appeared.

20. Garshin's italics.

21. Chekhov, *Pis'ma*, II, 331–32.

22. For the critical reception of "Pripadok," see Chekhov, *Sochineniia*, VII, 662–65.

23. Adolf Stender-Petersen, *Geschichte der Russischen Literatur* (History of Russian Literature) (Munich: Beck, 1957), II, 448. Stender-Petersen's italics.

24. L. A. Iezuitova, "Leonid Andreev i Vs. Garshin," *Vestnik Leningradskogo Universiteta: Seriia istorii, iazyka i literatury* 8(1964): 100.

Selected Bibliography

PRIMARY SOURCES

1. In Russian

Polnoe sobranie sochinenii (Complete Works). St. Petersburg: A. F. Marks, 1910.
Sochineniia (Works). *(Vstupitel'naia stat'ia, red. i kommentarii Ju. G. Oksmana).* Moscow: Gos. izdat. khudozh. lit., 1934.
Polnoe sobranie sochinenii. Pis'ma (Complete Works. Letters). *Red., stat'i i primechaniia Ju. G. Oksmana),* III. Moscow: Academiia, 1934.
Sochineniia (Works). *(Vstupitel'naia stat'ia i primechaniia G. A. Bialogo).* Moscow: Gos. izdat. khudozh. lit., 1955.
Sochineniia (Works). *(Vstupitel'naia stat'ia i primechaniia G. A. Bialogo).* Moscow: Gos. izdat. khudozh. lit., 1963.
Rasskazy (Short Stories). *(Vstupitel'naia stat'ia, podgotovka teksta i primechaniia S. Mashinskogo).* Moscow: "Sovetskaia Rossiia," 1976.

2. In English: Collections

The Signal and Other Stories. Trans. R. Smith. New York: Knopf, 1915. Reissued in Freeport, N.Y.: Books for Libraries Press, 1971. Contains all the stories with the exception of "The Artists."
The Scarlet Flower. Stories. Trans. B. Isaacs. Moscow: Foreign Language Publishing House, n.d. Contains all of Garshin's stories.

3. In English: Individual Stories

The three most famous stories and the anthologies or journals in which they appear are listed below.
"Four Days," in *Colorado Quarterly* 1(Summer 1972), Eugene Kayden, trans; in Graham, Stephan, ed. *Great Russian Short Stories.* New York: Liveright, 1929; in Guerney, B. G., ed. *The Portable Russian Reader.* New York: Viking, 1947; in Strahan, John, ed. *Fifteen Great Russian Short Stories.* New York: Washington Square Press, 1965.

"The Red Flower," in Chamot, Alfred, ed. *Selected Russian Short Stories.* London: Oxford, 1925; in *Colorado Quarterly* 3(Winter 1975), Eugene Kayden, trans., in Proffer, Carl, ed. *From Karamzin to Bunin: An Anthology of Russian Short Stories.* Bloomington: Indiana University Press, 1969; translated as "The Crimson Flower" in Graham, Stephan, ed. *Great Russian Short Stories.* New York: Liveright, 1929.

"The Signal," in Chamot, Alfred. *Selected Russian Short Stories.* London: Oxford, 1925; in *Colorado Quarterly* 1(Summer 1974), Eugene Kayden, trans; in Goodman, R. B., ed. *World-wide Short Stories.* New York: Globe Book Co., 1966; in Seltzer, Thomas, ed. *Best Russian Short Stories.* New York: The Modern Library, 1925.

SECONDARY SOURCES

1. In Russian

ABRAMOV, IAKOV, "V. M. Garshin: Materialy dlia biografii" (Garshin: Biographical Materials). In *Pamiati V. M. Garshina: Khudozh.-lit. sbornik* (In Memory of V. M. Garshin: Artistic and Literary Compilation). St. Petersburg: Shtein, 1889, pp. 1–65. Good biographical background material.

AIKHENVAL'D, IULII, (EICHENWALD). "Garshin." In *Siluety russkikh pisatelei* (Silhouettes of Russian Writers), 3rd. ed. Moscow: Izd. nauchnogo slova, 1911, I, 210–24. A good critical analysis of the inner workings of Garshin's stories.

ANDREEVSKII, SERGEI, "Vsevolod Garshin." *Russkaia mysl'* 6(1889): 46–64. A perceptive, thematic approach to the stories. Also some discussion of Tolstoy and Turgenev in relation to Garshin.

ARKHANGEL'SKII, VLADIMIR. "Osnovnoi obraz v tvorchestve Garshina" (The Basic Form in Garshin's Works). *Literatura i marksizm* 2(1929): 75–94. A discussion of typical traits of the Garshinian hero. At times overly propagandistic.

ARSEN'EV, KONSTANTIN. "V. M. Garshin i ego tvorchestvo" (V. M. Garshin and His Art). In Garshin, V. M. *Polnoe sobranie sochinenii.* St. Petersburg: A. F. Marks, 1910, pp. 525–39. A thoughtful and perceptive discussion of Garshin's stories by a contemporary critic.

BAZHENOV, NIKOLAI. "Dushevnaia drama Garshina" (Garshin's Spiritual Drama). *Russkaia mysl'* 1(1903): 34–52. An interesting though pretentious article by a psychiatrist who was also a literary critic.

BERDNIKOV, GEORGII. "Problema pessimizma. Chekhov i Garshin" (The Problem of Pessimism. Chekhov and Garshin). In *A. P. Chekhov: Ideinye i tvorcheskie iskaniia* (A. P. Chekhov: His Ideological and Artistic Quest). Moscow: Gos. izd. khudozh. lit., 1961, pp. 130–60. Good analysis of Garshin's stories in general. Discussion of Garshin and Chekhov in relation to "Pripadok" is particularly well done.

BIALYI, GRIGORII. *V. M. Garshin i literaturnaia bor'ba vos'midesiatykh godov* (V. M. Garshin and the Literary Struggle of the 1880s). Moscow: Izd. Akademii nauk SSSR, 1937. A thorough presentation of Garshin's works against the social, political, and historical events of the times.
————. *Vsevolod Garshin.* Leningrad: Prosveshchenie, 1969. Garshin's life and works discussed by a prolific Soviet expert on Garshin.
CHUKOVSKII, KORNEI. "O V. Garshine" (On V. Garshin). In Chukovskii, *Sobranie sochinenii.* Moscow: Izd. khudozh. lit., 1969, VI, 417–45. A good analytical discussion of Garshin's ability to depict the outer world of his characters.
EVNIN, FEDOR. "F. M. Dostoevskii i V. M. Garshin" (Dostoevsky and Garshin). *Izvestiia Akademii nauk SSSR: Otdelenie literatury i iazyka* 4(1962): 289–301. One of the few articles which discusses Dostoevsky's influence on Garshin.
FAUSEK, VIKTOR. "Vospominaniia" (Remembrances). In Garshin, V. M. *Polnoe sobranie sochinenii.* St. Petersburg: A. F. Marks, 1910, pp. 28–63. Interesting insights into Garshin's life and literary tastes by a close friend.
IAKUBOVICH, PETR. "Gamlet nashikh dnei" (Hamlet of Our Days). In Garshin, V. M. *Polnoe sobranie sochinenii.* St. Petersburg: A. F. Marks, 1910, pp. 539–50. A perceptive analysis of the major stories by a contemporary critic.
IEZUITOVA, L. A. "Leonid Andreev i Vs. Garshin" (Andreev and Garshin). *Vestnik Leningradskogo Universiteta: Seriia istorii, iazyka i literatury* 8(1964): 87–109. Garshin's influence on a well-known twentieth-century writer.
KLOCHKOVA, L. P. "Rukopisi i perepiska V. M. Garshina" (Garshin's Manuscripts and Correspondence). *Biulleteni rukopisnogo otdela Pushkinskogo doma* 8(1959): 45–114. A catalog of the material in the Garshin archives of the Academy of Sciences' Institute of Russian Literature.
KOROLENKO, VLADIMIR. "V. M. Garshin." In *Istoriia russkoi literatury XIX v.* (History of Nineteenth-Century Russian Literature), D. N. Ovsianiko-Kulikovskii, ed., 1910; rpt. The Hague: Mouton, 1969, IV, 335–61. A concise study of Garshin's life and works by a well-known writer and contemporary of Garshin's.
KOSTRSHCHITSA, VLADIMIR. "Deistvitel'nost', otrazhennaia v ispovedi" (Reality as Reflected in Confession). *Voprosy literatury* 12(1966): 135–44. A very good article, one of the very few dealing with Garshin's style.
MIKHAILOVSKII, NIKOLAI. "O Vsevolode Garshine" (On Garshin). In Mikhailovskii, *Polnoe sobranie sochinenii.* 2nd. ed. St. Petersburg: M. M. Stasiulevich, 1909, VI, 305–45. A detailed study of Garshin's works by one of the more prominent critics of the second half of the nineteenth century.

SHUVALOV, SERGEI. "Garshin-khudozhnik" (Garshin as Artist). In *V. M. Garshin,* ed. E. F. Nikitina. Moscow: Kooperativnoe izdatel'stvo pisatelei, 1931, pp. 103–26. An analysis of Garshin's literary technique including his use of similes and metaphors.

SKABICHEVSKII, ALEKSANDR. "V. M. Garshin." In *Istoriia noveishei russkoi literatury* (History of Recent Russian Literature). 5th ed. St. Petersburg: Obshchestvennaia pol'za, 1903, pp. 367–74. A fine discussion of Garshin's ability to depict the inner world of his characters.

SKVOZNIKOV, VASILII. "Realizm i romantizm v proizvedeniiakh V. M. Garshina" (Realism and Romanticism in Garshin's Writings). *Izvestiia Akademii nauk SSSR: Otdelenie literatury i iazyka* 16: 3(1957): 233–46. An intelligent and fairly impartial discussion of the coexistence of Realism and Romanticism in Garshin's stories.

2. In English

BRODAL, JAN. "The Pessimism of V. M. Garshin." *Scando-Slavica* 19(1973): 17–30. A discussion of pessimism as it relates to Garshin's life and works.

FETZER, LELAND. "Art and Assassination: Garshin's 'Nadezhda Nikolaevna.' " *Russian Review* 1(1975): 56–65. A good, though at times farfetched, discussion of Garshin's longest story.

KRAMER, KARL D. "Impressionist Tendencies in the Work of Vsevolod Garshin." *American Contributions to the Seventh International Congress of Slavists,* ed. Victor Terras. The Hague: Mouton, II, 339–55. An excellent analysis of Impressionism and its relevance to Garshin. One of the best articles on Garshin in English.

LEJINS, HAMILKARS. "Suicide in Garshin's Life and Stories." *South Central Bulletin* 4(1967): 34–44. Good discussion of an important topic.

MANNING, CLARENCE. "The Guilty Conscience of Garshin." *Slavonic Review* 29(1931): 285–92. The first article published in English on Garshin, but weak in subject matter.

PARKER, FAN. *Vsevolod Garshin: A Study of a Russian Conscience.* Morningside Heights, N.Y.: King's Crown Press, 1946. A seminal work in English, at times incisive, at times sentimental. Two chapters on Tolstoy and Garshin; some discussion of Garshin in relation to Hans Christian Andersen, Dostoevsky, and Turgenev.

SIEGEL, GEORGE. "The Art of Vsevolod Garshin." Diss. Harvard University, 1958. A rambling, digression-prone study which is perceptive and informative when the author sticks to the subject.

VARNAI, PAUL. "The Prose of V. Garshin." Diss. University of Michigan, 1970. Primarily an analysis of Garshin's use of narrative techniques, description, and dialogue.

————. "Structure and Syntactic Devices in Garshin's Stories." *Russian*

Language Journal 94/95(1972): 61–71. A short formalistic discussion of Garshin's use of structural and syntactical devices.

YARWOOD, EDMUND. "Hero and Foil: Structure in the Stories of V. Garshin." Diss. University of North Carolina, 1974. An analysis of the basic structure of the Garshinian short story. Also chapters on symbols used.

3. In German

GERICK, HORST-JÜRGEN. "Vsevolod M. Garshin als Vorläufer des russischen Symbolismus" (Garshin as a Forerunner of Russian Symbolism). *Die Welt der Slaven* 3(December 1962): 246–92. An excellent study of Garshin as a literary craftsman.

STENBORG, LENNART. *Studien zur Erzähltechnik in den Novellen V.M. Garshins* (Studies of Narrative Technique in the Stories of V. M. Garshin). Studia Slavica Upsaliensia, II. Uppsala: University of Uppsala, 1972. The most thorough study of Garshin's narrative techniques in any language. In general one of the finest studies of Garshin.

ZELM, ELLINOR. *Studien über Vsevolod Garshin* (Studies in Garshin). Published 1935; rpt. Nendeln/Liechtenstein: Kraus Reprint, 1968. Detailed study of Garshin's works as they relate to his life. Chapters on Garshin and his connection to Tolstoy, Hans Christian Andersen, and Charles Dickens.

Index

145